Cycle
ORKSHIRE

From road racing pioneers to
the ultimate Grand Départ and beyond

JONATHAN BROWN

GREAT NORTHERN

Great Northern Books Limited

PO Box 1380, Bradford, BD5 5FB

www.greatnorthernbooks.co.uk

For Laura, who I couldn't have done this without.

And in memory of my amazing mum, Allison Brown.

ISBN: 978-0-9933447-8-7

Design and layout: David Burrill

CIP Data

A catalogue for this book is available from the British Library

About the author

Jonathan Brown is an award-winning journalist who has worked for regional and national newspapers and currently works in broadcasting. During five years at the *Yorkshire Post* and *Yorkshire Evening Post* he worked as the Tour de France Grand Depart correspondent for both titles and covered subsequent Tour de Yorkshires as well as the ITU World Triathlon Series' visit to the county. While working on the Grand Depart he cycled the first stage of the 2014 Tour, delved into the region's cycling history and produced coverage from within the Tour's motorcade after riding pillion on a press bike through Yorkshire. He currently lives and works in Leeds.

Acknowledgements

Thank you to everyone who agreed to be interviewed, the Yorkshire cycling community, Welcome to Yorkshire, Yorkshire Post Newspapers and Great Northern Books.

CONTENTS

FOREWORD

SIR GARY VERITY

(Richard Walker/www.imagenorth.net)

It is hugely gratifying to know that Yorkshire is now regarded as the home of cycling within the UK, and that it has garnered a world-class reputation within the sport. Four million fans lined the route when the Tour de France visited the county in 2014 and race director Christian Prudhomme famously hailed it "the grandest of Grand Départs".

Since then I have been proud to oversee the launch of the Tour de Yorkshire – a race which is now regarded as one of the most dramatic and well-supported events on the calendar – and it still gives me goosebumps whenever I see masses of cyclists lining our county's roads.

Certainly, Yorkshire's relationship with the bike is not a new one, as this book more than aptly shows. We have a rich history of producing trailblazing talents like Brian Robinson, Barry Hoban and Beryl Burton, and Ben Swift, Ed Clancy and Lizzie Deignan have all become World Champions in recent years.

Our stunning yet uncompromising landscape has undoubtedly played a part in this, and with the possible exception of hors-catégorie mountains, we have everything a cyclist could wish for. Yorkshire possesses mile after mile of quiet country lanes on which athletes can easily hone their skills, endless rolling hills, short-sharp ascents, and a sprinkling of cobbles thrown in for good measure.

The weather also breeds an innate toughness needed to prosper, as do those traditional Yorkshire character traits of honesty, persistency, hard work and ambition. This production line of talented riders shows no signs of stopping either and there are many youngsters out there right now working hard to follow in these illustrious footsteps.

Fireworks light up the sky above Leeds Town Hall in celebration of Yorkshire winning the right to host the 2014 Tour de France Grand Départ. January 17 2013. (Bruce Rollinson, Yorkshire Post Newspapers)

Why cycling?

People often ask me why Welcome to Yorkshire chose cycling as a vehicle to promote our great county on the world stage.

For me it was obvious – sport has a unique ability to transcend social barriers, and what better sport than cycling to showcase our wares?

I already had a longstanding passion for the sport, and recognised the inimitable opportunities it presented. Daily television coverage typically lasts for three to four hours and the sweeping helicopter shots act like a rolling postcard for the county. And while the racing might not always provide an edge-of-your-seat intensity, those lulls in the action give commentators the opportunity to take in the surroundings and chat about the outstanding features along the route.

In 2016 the Tour de Yorkshire was broadcast in 178 countries and attracted a global audience of 11.4 million viewers – that's an awful lot of people welcoming Yorkshire into their homes. And we must not forget those two million joyous spectators who lined the race route. No other sporting event could generate such a mammoth attendance, and the boost that had on our economy was unparalleled, with independent research noting a £60 million boost in income.

One figure that can't be measured however is the role these races have come to play in our local communities. The way they have brought people of all ages, backgrounds and beliefs together is one of our very proudest achievements, and it never ceases to impress me when I see towns and villages lined with flags, banners and bunting when the peloton passes through. Yorkshire folk have taken cycling to their hearts and cemented our reputation as one of the greatest race destinations on earth. With the 2019 UCI Road World Championships on the horizon, the return of the Tour de France looking likely, and the Tour de Yorkshire growing year on year, the future certainly looks rosy as well.

Of course, none of this would have been possible without those Yorkshire cycling icons like the ones featured in this book. When you talk to the legends of the sport like Eddy Merckx and Bernard Hinault, they remember the exploits of our most famous exports, and for that we owe them a great debt of gratitude.

That is why I'm delighted Jonathan has brought together their stories, and chronicled Yorkshire's longstanding love affair with the bike. That relationship has not always been an easy one – as the accounts of Sid Barras and Chris Walker attest to in the wider context of the sport – but right now that connection has never been stronger and this, to me, is an enthralling and comprehensive account of how we got here today.

PROLOGUE

The eyes of the world are on Yorkshire and I'm at the epicentre of a storm of flashing lenses and roaring crowds.

The biggest bike race on the planet has made its way across the Channel to launch from the North of England for the first time. The Tour de France is starting here, in Leeds.

It's the world's most watched sporting event, beamed out to 3.5billion people across the globe every year, but at the start line on The Headrow I'm not the only one who has no idea what to expect. Hundreds of thousands of people have packed into the city centre to wave off 198 fine-tuned athletes on their three-week long 3,700km challenge.

On the surface it's simply a PR masterstroke. Literally billions are about to see the county's defining weekend on TV, while millions more will see it speed past their front doors.

But this is also a homecoming: Yorkshire's long overdue weekend in the limelight after six decades of graft and innovation. Within the crowds of flag-waving fans and ecstatic spectators are dozens of ex-pro cyclists, whose years of churning the pedals while battling against the sporting odds, have paved the way for the most special of occasions ever to grace the White Rose county; a seminal weekend in their own stories.

Most of those men and women would give their right arm to experience the inner-workings of the Tour de France's immense juggernaut of pounding legs, twisting cogs and tensioned chains; but, for reasons unknown to me, I've been blessed with the opportunity to see it from within.

The vast race's media men hand me a helmet and pass me over to one of the great race's 'pilots' – a Toulouse motorcyclist named Gaetan Prime. I have two days of breathtaking action ahead, riding pillion on a media motorbike handled by a likeable extrovert who's riding British roads for the first time and barely speaks a word of English.

Within seconds of our introduction, I'm speeding up Scott Hall Road through north Leeds hanging on to the back of the bike as if my life depends on it. We shift through the gears at the centre of a hallowed path marked out by thousands of technicolor fans at either side of the road; some jumping, most cheering and even more waving with smiles plastered across their faces –

not for the peloton of global stars who are miles behind, but for a pair of anonymous blokes on a motorbike. Now that's a pure Yorkshire welcome.

Racing ahead of the Tour's cycling thoroughbreds from the start, Gaetan and his colleagues whip up the crowd, pipping their horns and gesturing at fans like warm-up acts for the main event. I can't help but get involved; we wave back at the swarms of roadside smiles, lean over for high-fives, stop for pictures, share our packed lunches and chat with people waiting to see the stars of one of the world's toughest races – every single face beaming back and up for a natter.

We spend as much time high-fiving excited kids on their dads' shoulders as we do grandmas; and it's not just the media bikes. The French Gendarmerie, race officials and even Yorkshire police play for the crowd. All this excitement, and the time section of the first stage hasn't even started yet as we roll past Harewood and wait for the nod over the race radio that the stopwatch has started for the 2014 Tour de France. Soon enough we're given the green light, Gaetan waits for the peloton and then snaps back into action.

We power through Wharfedale,

The Tour de France peloton makes its way past York Minster on the second day of the 2014 Tour de France. July 6 2014. (Jonathan Gawthorpe, YPN)

pass the roaring crowds that have packed into Skipton town centre under the shadow of the yellow jersey that dons Skipton Castle for the day, and enter the Yorkshire Dales. Only three media motorbikes are allowed to get up close to the riders at any moment, so we bide our time. Well, we do until we run out of fuel near Threshfield, prompting a mad scramble to fill up the bike at a closed petrol station that the locals reopen just for us as Gaetan tries and fails to pay in Euros. It's a sign of things to come.

We launch out of the village, passing a gleefully welcoming Napoleon impersonator on the way, until we're waved back to meet a small breakaway of riders outside Kettlewell; you can see every bead of sweat. But my glimpse at the hypnotic fluidity of the lead riders is short-lived as we're ushered forward for safety reasons along the sharp turns and compact lanes of the Yorkshire countryside.

Flying up the climbs beneath the whirring blades of the TV helicopters above, we're given a tiny pathway by vibrant hordes of international fans desperately hoping to pat their Tour heroes on the back as they grind their way to the summits. The remote hills are more densely populated than they ever have been. And all anyone wants to do is have a good time and get the best view they can; some are even looking down from cherry pickers or the raised scoops of diggers.

From the accordion music and fancy dress fans bejewelled with garlic and false moustaches to the man with an inflatable mackerel that he's called 'Malcolm' atop Buttertubs, the festival mood is infectious. En route we've already been offered a glass of Pimms, given a sombrero and serenaded, all in the name of Le Tour.

The only bump in the road comes when Gaetan motions that he's stopping to wait by the roadside between stage one climbs but skids on a patch of mud beside a farmer's gate. We both instinctively launch the proverbial ejector seat and somehow manage to land on our feet and rescue the bike. It's a non-stop rush.

The close call with the tarmac pales into insignificance as we near Harrogate. The welcome is truly jaw-dropping – thousands upon thousands of people everywhere you turn roaring at the mere sight of motion along the route. Even affable Gaetan is stunned into silence.

During stage two we get even closer to the action, and more often. I meet Gaetan on the start line at York Racecourse and we set off from the pavilion through the rammed streets of the medieval city.

Following an early seven-rider break from the pack, we get a chance to hang back. Gaetan tucks between the breakaway and the mass peloton, with yellow jersey-clad Marcel Kittel up front, near Starbeck.

I'm looking over my shoulder straight into Kittel's reflective glasses and then we reach a wide roundabout. The peloton splits either side of it before merging as if swallowing it whole.

Mesmerised, I'm desperate to see more, so we again tuck in front of the peloton as they complete Cragg Vale's long, gradual ascent. We coast along, just metres from the world's greatest cyclists until suddenly I'm thrust back and holding on for dear life. A stern race official shouts us on, and I turn to see a wave of Tour elite chasing us at over 40mph, snaking through Huddersfield's streets lined 10-deep with fans. I've seldom been so scared, leaning tight into the corners, my helmet whistling past the blurs of cheering crowds. Gaetan has it under control.

He doesn't even seem phased at the immense swarm of people zigzagging up Holme Moss and forming a metre-wide path for us. He tucks in his wing mirrors shouting "Bonjour, ca va" while I tense up fearing the worst. It's all part of the race.

The adrenaline high is constant throughout the leans and dips we take on the motorbike. The finish – after the best part of 10 hours on the solid saddle of Gaetan's Tour Kawasaki over two days – still comes too soon. I hop off the bike like new-born Bambi, not used to using my legs, and take to my tiptoes to see Vincenzo Nibali distance himself from the rest in a sprint to take victory on stage two in Sheffield.

It has been the grandest of Grand Départs. It's meant fun and frolics for most, and something far deeper and more significant for the people of Yorkshire who have lived through the highs and lows of British cycling. The tears of joy shed on July 5th and 6th weren't just for seeing their home county at its beautiful, inspiring best, but for the 60-year mountain that White Rose road racing has had to climb to reach this point.

What a race, what a sport, what a county. A watershed weekend in a rollercoaster journey.

Brian Robinson signing autographs during his first Tour de France in 1955. (YPN)

THE PIONEER

Cycling was more than a sport during the Second World War; it was a way of life.

Petrol and food were being rationed, families had relatives bravely fighting abroad and those who stayed back in England were put to work by clearing up the twisted metal and debris from German air raids or by working shifts in mills converted into military production lines.

Ravensthorpe teenager Brian Robinson summed up a generation of Yorkshire folk, who didn't so much as love cycling but lived it amid the tales of death, disaster and Nazi warmongering of the 1940s. The uncertainty and fear that had engulfed Britain and Yorkshire at the time had also fostered a sense of togetherness in tough times, and opened the door to a natural need for escapism when it was almost impossible to avoid stories of tragedy and loss.

Robinson was studying a trade qualification at technical college as a 13-year-old, while mucking in at home and helping his joiner father in any way he could. His dad had been exempt from National Service because he was classed as a skilled tradesman and played his part during the conflict by driving wagons transporting supplies between railway stations and military depots. Robinson senior also took his son to Sheffield to clear the mangled wreckages of city buildings destroyed during the Blitz.

Brian Robinson. June 21 2010. (YPN)

Meanwhile, other members of the family worked in West Yorkshire cotton mills that had been converted into factories producing parts for Halifax bomber aeroplanes. It was all hands to the pump.

Outside college, where he was working towards following in his dad's practical footsteps, Brian tended to the family allotment with his older brother Des as they tried to help the family cope with the rigours and poverty of war. They were a frugal unit, a hard-working bunch.

But amid the relentless graft, a sporting seed was planted. Cycling had always been in the background – his dad and brother were keen riders in his youth – but the war exposed the teenager to the joys of the open road as the trio cycled the often barren, traffic-free roads from their home via Leeds and Wharfedale to visit family near Harrogate. They would sprint to beat each other to signposts along the way and the kick of adrenaline he got from racing and flying down hills on two wheels soon enraptured him. Cycling became a welcome distraction from a hand-to-mouth existence; whizzing across fields and along paths on his shortcuts to college with the wind running through his hair became a daily highlight.

Those initial thrills and spills eventually inspired him to join junior rides at the Huddersfield Road Club, which had counted Des and his father as members over the years. Now in his mid 80s – but still as passionate as ever about the bike – he told me: "We've got the magic terrain really. From where I am, once you've cleared the town you're in the countryside. But it didn't catch my imagination to start with; I did it because of my brother. We had to wait until 14 to join a club and then we participated to the limit."

Although his father banned him from competing in organised races until he turned 18, Brian still immersed himself in the popular pursuit of group club rides through the White Rose's undulating countryside with members of the Huddersfield outfit. He clung to the back wheels of the older lads – his brother three years his senior – before evolving into an accomplished clubman at home in Yorkshire's lauded Dales and the high Peak District that lay within cycling distance of his doorstep. The 100-mile rides would send them looping around places like Ripon and Matlock Bath every week; the famed Holme Moss ascent – for which he held the hill climb record at six minutes and five seconds for years – becoming part of his cycling routine.

Robinson was just one of thousands of Yorkshire youngsters falling in love with a sport that made the most of the region's natural landscape, taking them away from the grind of their day-to-day lives. They grew up in a thoroughly working-class region, punctuated by the mineshafts, steelworks and mills that had brought the area to prominence during the industrial revolution but had struggled during the recession of the late 1930s. Cars were far from commonplace and roads outstripped demand. It was an open invitation issued to a generation to explore the beauty of Yorkshire's remote, far-flung gems at pace astride a bicycle.

"As a youngster I always wanted a motorbike," Brian told me. "It was war time and it was a no-no really so getting a bike was the next best thing. If you wanted to get anywhere it would be by bike."

Despite the climate at the time, cycling in a group in organised races in England was actually banned. It followed an infamous incident that was to play a part in shaping the progress of British bike racing internationally; or the lack of it. Around the turn of the century the UK found itself completely at odds with the status quo of cycling in mainland Europe and the two opposing approaches to the sport created a deep rift that took decades to repair.

Immense cross-country road races covering the length and breadth of entire countries emerged as the ultimate tests of man and machine during the very early days of cycling experimentation. The most testing distance races were in France. The mammoth Paris-Brest-Paris race, in which a group of riders took on a 750-mile course – seven-times the length of some modern day Tour de France stages – all in one go, was launched in 1891, as was the similarly-lengthy Bordeaux-Paris. These long-haul timed races flourished and became the norm on the continent, many developing into the one-day 'Classics' races that the world's greatest cyclists have coveted ever since.

The Grand Tours – the Tour de France, Vuelta a España (Tour of Spain) and Giro d'Italia (Tour of Italy) – were established at the start of the 20th Century, offering riders a different type of endurance challenge. Cyclists were asked to compete in a series of massed-start races – also known as 'bunched' races – over three week periods, with the overall winner being the rider who completed all the individual races in the shortest combined time. The overall winner was awarded the leader's jersey – which for instance is yellow in the Tour de France – in a tradition that is now embedded in all international stage races. Prizes for the best performing sprint cyclists, climbers and young riders over the three weeks were also brought in later.

Initially, Brits ventured across the Channel to compete in these blossoming bike races but an incident back home changed everything, and cracks began to appear between the way cyclists competed in Britain and the rest of Europe. In 1894, riders taking part in a 50-mile race out of London spooked a horse that was pulling a lady in a carriage. The horse bolted, the carriage ended up in a ditch and the woman involved complained to the police. The country's cycling body, the National Cycling Union (NCU), stepped in to avoid the police banning cyclists from British roads entirely by barring riders from taking part in all forms of racing on public roads in a move that ushered racers towards tracks so that cycling commuters would not be affected.

The ban eventually led to the rise of track racing and what later became known as time trialling – where cyclists set off on the same course a short distance apart in a bid to set the fastest time. Key players in a rival UK cycling body, the Road Records Association, created a new code of practice so that secret time trials could take place on isolated country lanes without attracting the attention of the police. Riders dressed fully in black, wearing no race numbers, would set off alone on the same agreed course, starting at short time intervals. If a rider was caught by another competitor, they immediately had to drop back so that the racers were at no time riding in bunches.

The secrecy saved cycle racing in the UK from oblivion but the state of play put British riders at a huge disadvantage to their continental counterparts. Time trialling – often described as the 'race of truth' – is solely reliant on a rider's ability to negotiate a course against the elements and, of course, the clock. Bunched road racing, however, allows riders to work together in packs and save energy. The leading riders punch a hole in the air for those sat further back in the group, or 'peloton', who are therefore shielded from the wind and only need to expend as little as half the energy of the riders ahead to keep up. The tactical, team element of massed-start racing soon became an alien concept for British cyclists. And as British-based riders ducked and dived to enjoy cycling as amateurs, many successful continental riders were able to make a living as cyclists in what was a growing sport flush with sponsorship. The divide between Britain and the rest of Europe following the ban meant it would be 50 years until a British cyclist won a major race on the continent.

For the likes of Brian Robinson back in the White Rose, the entrenched divide in sporting politics was of little concern; he just loved riding his bike. After the war ended his family moved the short distance to Mirfield in West Yorkshire and Robinson senior bought a joinery firm of his own, with Brian starting a seven-year apprenticeship under his watchful eye. The hard work would continue. The firm's workshop helped with much-needed local house repairs as the recovery effort following Nazi bombardment moved up a level. The Robinsons also used their joinery skills to double up as coffin makers. Taking over the duties of funeral directors carried the bonus of a petrol allowance during a continued period of post-war rationing, which boosted the family coffers. It wasn't a glamourous pursuit but it paid the bills.

By 1949 Brian was 19 and working while competing on the club circuit, giving it some welly on his trusty bike every Sunday; often cycling huge distances to get to his races before competing and cycling home. The celebrated Manx Cycling Week on the Isle of Man, which attracted some of the world's top talent, was the only official massed-start road racing event in Britain at the time and it became an annual family holiday for the

Robinsons. Crucially, it also gave the brothers an early glimpse of what the European pros were made of. Otherwise time trials and bunched races on closed circuits became the norm week-in, week-out.

Cycling in Britain was still considered an amateur sport dominated by the working class, while tales of folklore and legend were being written by the likes of Fausto Coppi, who was putting in the miles in tactical continental massed-start races as pros. Brian Robinson, meanwhile, was working six days a week as a joiner in Mirfield and riding for pleasure. "It was after hours really," he said. "We did our 48 and a half hours at work and then it was bikes all week. In the winter we worked till 5pm on site so we could have our mornings off in the summer to make time for training. You worked during the week like everyone else and then on a Sunday you got on your bike and rode as fast as you could; it really was as simple as that."

It was a simple obsession for Robinson in what were simple times. Hard graft on a bike came as naturally as working his knuckles to the bone for his dad, and as he sprinted into his 20s, life was to take a turn that would have an impact far wider than he could have imagined.

Robinson's break in international cycling came through an unlikely source: National Service with the King's Own Light Infantry. The 21-year-old, who had been given a bike in his first sponsorship deal with the Ellis Briggs bike shop of Shipley just three months earlier, was ordered to report for duty at Strensall Barracks in York in January 1952. His two-year stint had been put back so that he could complete his apprenticeship, so his arrival at Strensall had been somewhat of a lurking spectre as his enjoyable hobby was fast turning into a part-time job. Robinson, of course, arrived for duty on his bike and after six weeks of basic training, he angled his way into the army's cycling team.

His brother Des was also progressing as a cyclist and was highly rated by the NCU at the time. The governing body's endorsement saw him sent on a training camp run by a French bicycle component manufacturer in the South of France in the early 1950s. The experience blew his mind; he met veterans of the Tour de France, tested himself on French mountains and brought home copies of dedicated French cycling magazines. The imagery and infectious excitement opened Brian's eyes to the world of cycling beyond British time trialling – a side of the sport he never really enjoyed. Cycling was done differently on the continent, it was more glamorous and was uncharted land as far as he was concerned.

The eye-opener brought home the magnitude of the world's biggest cycling spectacle, the Tour de France, which was founded in 1903 partly as a vanity project aimed at boosting the circulation of French sports newspaper L'Auto. As such, it was a publicity-hungry beast that boasted the best riders and the most challenging bunched racing in the world over three punishing weeks. It had evolved from its rag-tag early days of underhand tactics and shortcuts to become a gruelling test of individual strength. Rules were so tough in fact that riders were allowed no mechanical support during its early years, meaning they would have spare tyres looped around their shoulders and were banned from discarding any equipment during consecutive stages that could last up to 250 miles.

The Tour had come back bigger and better than ever in 1947 after an eight-year hiatus prompted by the outbreak of war. It was now affiliated with the newspaper L'Equipe, as it still is today, and was seen as a symbol of France's rebirth following the devastation of World War Two. It was a rolling PR parade. Meanwhile, back in Britain home-based riders were no longer subject to the same undercover racing rules as previously but the NCU's continual unwillingness to budge from its ban of massed-start road races led to the foundation of the British League of Racing Cyclists (BLRC). The new organisation set about organising bunched races on British public roads after talks with police in the early 1940s, and sparked a battle of ideologies that would last 20 years. The divide was initially so entrenched that anyone even so much as competing in a BLRC event would be banned by the NCU, which also made them unavailable for selection as Team GB riders in major events like the Olympics or Commonwealth Games.

Robinson towed the line without upsetting the governing body but was eyeing up the opportunity to test himself against the best as his regimented army lifestyle increased his fitness and prepared him for the world outside his home county. He remembers it well: "It got me out the house, it taught me domestic skills and how to live and survive on my own. It was good for me. In the army you learn to fight for yourself, it's a bit selfish really."

Having, alongside his draughtsman brother, been singled out as a potential GB rider for the 1952 Helsinki Olympic road race, Brian and a handful of army cycling team members were selected to take part in the Route de France – an amateur stage race for riders considered capable of riding the Tour de France in the future – as part of a joint army-NCU team. The race, involving experienced teams of young road racers from Holland, Italy, France and Belgium, was a baptism of fire for Brian. The French-speaking pack and Pyrenean mountains, known as 'Cols', were a world away from anything he'd experienced before. Unknowingly riding at the foot of the notorious ascent of the near-7,000ft Col du Tourmalet, Brian struggled to conceive peaks that made the Dales look like mole hills. "We were riding on the flat near Bordeaux and I could see flashing way on up in the sky," he said. "I asked one of the guys next to me what the lights were in pigeon French; it was the sunshine flashing on car windscreens. I got to comprehend that we were going up there and I thought 'oh blimey'. We've got Holme Moss in England and it's nothing compared to that. My record on Holme Moss is just over six minutes and it takes an hour to get up the Cols. It was a question of survival really and seeing what the other guys did."

Following a huge effort, Brian completed the gruelling Route de France; his fatigue a stark illustration of the chasm that needed to be bridged if he were to make it on the continent as a road racer. Still in recovery mode, Brian, Des and another Brit boarded a plane bound for Helsinki to compete in the 1952 Olympic Games. They rode against men including Jacques Anquetil, who would later win an unprecedented five Tours de France, within a bunch of riders that finished 50 yards down on the eventual winner. His mind was made up, he was going to ride the Tour de France despite the fact that only two Brits before him had ever attempted it and both had abandoned before the end.

Following a further year of cycling during his national service, with NCU and BLRC in-fighting continuing, Brian went back to work for his dad's joinery firm in 1953 and raced domestically before getting signed up by the British-based Hercules team as a fully-fledged pro in 1955. Despite having barely any experience of the rigours of continental racing, the team set up shop in the South of France with the ambitious aim of entering a Great Britain team in the Tour de France, which was at the time contested by national outfits along with several French regional teams. This was Brian's chance; he was determined to make the transition to European racing at a time when life in Yorkshire was quite insular. He was prepared to sacrifice home comforts to follow his dream. Intent on integrating in France, he set himself the target of learning one sentence of French every single day.

He told me: "I wanted to race abroad more than anything else; everything else was secondary. I had no problems with the food, the language was a problem to start with but we got over that. For me, to think you could come from the backstreets of Yorkshire and be on the top starts in France was unusual but I never had any reservations about being away from home. I used to come back twice a year. I wasn't like one of the lads who used to say 'I'm dying for my mother's Yorkshire pudding'. I just lived the life of a biker."

He fared well in major stage race Paris-Nice, known as the 'race to the sun',

The Mirfield man (centre) competing in the 1956 Tour de France. (PA/PA Archive/PA Images)

placing eighth overall, before taking part in the seven-day Tour de Sud-Est where he wore the leader's jersey for a day. Learning the tactics and strategies – where to stay in the bunch, which splinter groups of breakaway riders to ignore and when to launch an attack – of the multi-stage events were all part of an intense learning curve that few Britons had exposed themselves to before. But Brian was adjusting on and off the bike in what was a completely new type of apprenticeship; one for which there was simply no blueprint to follow.

"Being on the breadline helped," he said. "It toughened you up to start with. Riding a bike isn't easy, you need a couple of weeks to get used to it. It's a bit of a shock to the system. There were some people that came up the easy way but they didn't endure."

That first GB Tour de France team, backed by Hercules, was a relatively tight-knit group by all accounts; all 10 riders willing to cooperate in the goal of finishing the 22-stage Tour of 1955. But they were grossly ill-prepared. The jagged, slippery cobbles, or 'pave', of Northern France and Belgium

Robinson claims third in the 1957 edition of Milan-San Remo. (YPN)

chiselled away at the inexperienced by testing stamina and bike handling early on. The incessant heat, mammoth Cols, punctures, crashes and exhaustion eventually whittled the British team down to two solitary cyclists: Robinson and Hampshire plumber Tony Hoar. The pair rolled over the line in Paris as pioneers. Robinson finished 29th ahead of Hoar, who finished in last place, making him the first Briton ever to complete a Tour de France. He had passed an almighty test and in doing so laid the foundations for generations of British riders in the toughest sporting spectacle on the planet.

Spending eight months of the year out in France and travelling Europe as a continental road racer became Brian's routine, making a large portion of his earnings – providing he had done well in big races such as the Tour – through late summer round-the-town criterium circuit races where popular riders drew big fees. A Yorkshire grafter at heart, Brian would then come home every September, getting his hands dirty for the family firm doing everything from building work to dressing corpses for funerals.

For the start of the new season, following the thrashing its riders received in the '55 Tour, the British-based Hercules team disbanded. In its absence, Brian was allowed to join a 'Luxembourg and the rest' team led by famed climber and Luxembourger Charly Gaul; a man fittingly known as the 'Angel of the Mountains' for the way he glided up ascents. Robinson, gaining many plaudits along the way, finished in 14th behind team leader Gaul in 13th in 1956. But the story of that Tour for Robinson was one of his team's internal fractions. It became clear that succeeding in the event, known in France as 'Le Grand Boucle', is nigh on impossible without proper support from your teammates; a fact that would halt the progress of pioneering riders with Yorkshire coursing through their veins for years to come.

"In the Tour you went in as an individual and you knew you weren't going to get a place in the general classification (overall lead)," Brian remembered. "You played the field as long as you did something to get contracts elsewhere like win a stage. You're a professional and live on what you earn and that's what you need. Charly's guys did what he wanted. We would all agree that if anybody punctured in the first 100km three of us would stop to help, but after that you were on your own."

The national team format, which laboured through until 1961, put Robinson and others from countries that were minorities in the Tour at a huge disadvantage in those early days. A Tour de France simply cannot be won by one man alone; a point illustrated by the fact that most team leaders pledged to share their prize money among their teammates to garner support. No matter how plucky Yorkshire's pioneers were back then, there was a ceiling to their success.

The format did not bode well for team spirit either. Riders raced for sponsored multinational trade teams all year round, including in the Tours of Spain and Italy, but were divided into national outfits solely for the Tour de France and the World Championships one-day road race later in the year. It meant trade teammates could find themselves competing against each other in the biggest race of all, forcing riders to choose between national loyalties and staying on good terms with the trade teams which paid their wages.

Aside from the politics, Robinson's strong start left him in a good position for 1957. He and his wife Shirley drove down to the South of France and parked up their caravan for the duration of a pre-season training camp with the trade team St Raphael-Geminiani for which he would work relentlessly to make ends meet. The Tour may have been the pinnacle of the sport but the glitz and glamour of European pro racing in the 1950s was largely superficial. Riders had to work immensely hard just to maintain their place in the pro ranks. There could be no such thing as burnout.

The Italian Classic 'Milan San-Remo' remains one of the five most prized single-day continental races in professional cycling – the Tour of Flanders, Paris-Roubaix, Liège-Bastogne-Liège and the Tour of Lombardy are the others. Those giants of the cycling calendar are fittingly known as the 'Monuments'. Given its prestige and Robinson's humble roots, his third place in Milan-San Remo 1957 put his name in the top bracket as he fought ahead of 220 other riders including the likes of Anquetil and the legendary Louison Bobet. It was an historic podium for Brian that proved a high-point in the build-up to an ultimately fruitless Tour de France in which he retired after stage four due to a wrist injury. The best was yet to come.

Robinson's European fairytale progressed yet further in the '58 Tour, although his moment of glory wasn't quite what he had envisaged. Riding for a new 'Internations' team, which included two other Brits and talented Irishman Shay Elliott, Brian found himself in another divided setup from the offset. The team leader, Austrian Adolf Christian, refused to split his winnings if he won the Tour overall, prompting a familiar every-man-for-himself rift.

The divisions made things difficult but Robinson was a rare breed; a Yorkshireman who had embraced every aspect of continental racing, living in France and dedicating himself to learning and speaking the native language at every turn. During his time on the Internations team of '58, he and his teammate Elliott abandoned their mother tongue unlike their monolingual compatriots. They were immersed in a mission to become European success stories despite the obvious obstacles in front of them.

And regardless, competing for only themselves and the few other allies they had within the team did have its advantages. In 1958 it allowed Brian to pinpoint the 170km stage seven ride from Saint-Brieuc to Brest as a chance for him to stand out from his so-called teammates. The undulating countryside course mirrored the hills of his home county and came ahead of a time trial that many of the big hitters were already looking at saving their energy for. Powering away from the peloton after 50km with a French rider and the Italian cyclist Arigo Padovan, he stayed with the Italian all the way to the line to set up a dramatic sprint finish. With 400 metres to go, Padovan was slightly ahead when Brian attacked but was twice squeezed into the spectators by his tiring rival, who crossed the line in front. Padovan's

A picture of relief after completing a Tour de France.

foul play saw him demoted and Britain had its first Tour de France stage win in history.

Robinson had done it; a Yorkshire joiner had put British cycling on the map. Word spread back home, even filtering on to the pages of a national press that rarely looked beyond football, horse racing, rugby and cricket. And although his Tour ended prematurely after succumbing to dysentery, diarrhoea and exhaustion following stage 19, Brian's landmark victory had broken down barriers. He had been robbed of his moment of glory by Padovan, so his next mission was to leave Europe in no doubt as to his ability.

By 1959, Brian Robinson was an established name. A respected member of the peloton, a proven team player for his trade team and a man armed with the ability to compete with the best in continental Classics and stage

Brian Robinson pictured with one of his vintage jerseys and bikes in April 2014. (Tony Johnson, YPN)

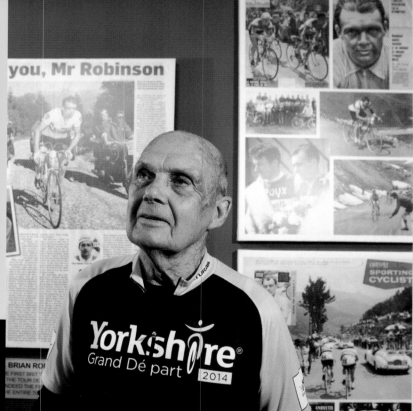

Pictured at a gallery displaying his sporting achievements. (YPN)

races. But claiming a stage victory in the Tour de France of that year was never going to be easy. Having suffered with a recurring stomach complaint days earlier, Brian was coaxed through 231km of torture during stage 19 from Aurillac to Clermont-Ferrand by Elliott. The Irishman nursed his struggling pal up ascents, sheltered him from the wind, plied him with water and even gave him the odd supporting shove which eventually landed both riders with a fine. They finished 47 minutes down on the leaders, prompting an end to Elliott's Tour as he had finished outside the time limit – the winner's finishing time plus a percentage that depends on the difficulty of the stage. Elliott had sacrificed himself.

Robinson, on the other hand, avoided the chop due to a loophole that stated that any rider who started the day in the top 10 overall did not have to finish within the same time limit. It seemed that the gesture by Elliott, who was admittedly not a strong climber, came because he thought Brian would have a better chance in the Alpine stages to come. He was right.

Having regained his strength, Robinson took on the 202km stage 20 slog from Annecy to Chalon-sur-Saône with a real sense of optimism. He had the mechanic fit lightweight time trial wheels and decided he would aim for a solo breakaway, where a single rider escapes from the clutches of the peloton in an audacious bid for victory. Knowing the course, he made his break ahead of a steep climb and never looked back. Brian initially had French climber Jean Dotto for company but eventually broke free on his own through an imperious mountain descent with 140km left to go. Brian repaid Elliott's faith by finishing a stunning 20 minutes ahead of the pack. It was the moment of individual glory he had earned and deserved.

Robinson's impressive staying power and continental success was filtering through to the enthusiasts at home. Suddenly competing in the world's biggest bike race seemed attainable. During that '59 Tour, Robinson was joined by a small group of aspiring continental road racers from Britain – partly thanks to his example and partly as remnants of the Hercules British team of four years earlier tried again.

Vic Sutton, a skinny boat builder from Doncaster, was one of those to race alongside Robinson and he made a big impression. He famously led a trio of Tour winners – Anquetil (1957), Gaul (1958) and Federico Bahamontes who went on to win in 1959 – up the same Col du Tourmalet that had once mystified Robinson; showing a glimpse of natural talent that would never fully be realised. He had set off for France with Tony Hewson, from Sheffield, and Londoner John Andrews a year earlier in a war-time ambulance that they had converted into a makeshift mobile home. They settled in Reims, had their expenses paid by a local club and were desperate to prove themselves. Places in the '59 Tour beckoned but, while his pals had both retired by stage seven, Sutton jumped from group to group up the famous Pyrenean Col to earn plaudits from the admiring French press.

Sutton's stunning climb was followed by a tentative descent down the mountain, which saw him drop down the field. But his efforts elevated him from a backmarker in 109th to 37th overall by the time the Tour reached the finish line in Paris. He was even billed as having the potential to be the next Charly Gaul prior to the following year's Tour but collapsed after a tough stage in the Alps. He had an undiagnosed heart problem and was told he should never race again. Sutton quit professionally but returned to the bike in his 60s during the 1990s, tragically dying in a veterans' race in 1999 after his heart gave up the fight. Sutton's promise gave another, albeit fleeting, glimpse of what riders reared on Yorkshire's summits could do.

Robinson took part in two further Tours de France. He finished 26th as nominal leader of the 1960 Great Britain team and 53rd while racing for his country the next year.

At the age of 33, a year before his retirement, Brian made sure he left the world of pro cycling with a sign of what he might have achieved with better support. In the twilight of his career, he scored an overall victory in the 1961 Criterium du Dauphine-Libere. The seven-stage event is a highly respected continental race during the build-up to the Tour de France. Unlike the Tour, the Dauphine was contested by trade teams, meaning Brian would be working with his Rapha-Gitane teammates. Well backed by his fellow pros, he established a lead and never looked like losing it.

Brian Robinson, a shrewd and focused man with a plan, set the bar for Britons cycling abroad; but there was a new kid on the block who was to raise it even further.

Tom Simpson.
February 5 1967. (PA)

MAJOR SIMPSON

A gangly 21-year-old Northern lad was introduced to Brian Robinson during the 1959 Tour de France. The youngster was due to negotiate a contract with Brian's trade team; and for more money than the veteran.

Taken aback but nevertheless graciously helpful, Brian translated between amateur Tom Simpson and his St Raphael trade team boss Raymond Louviot at the British Tour team's hotel when the race stopped in Brittany. Brian knew instantly from Louviot's attitude that this kid was something special.

Tom Simpson was a miner's son from Harworth, a village south of Doncaster on the border with Nottinghamshire, who had been racing as an independent – not affiliated with a pro trade team but could race in both amateur and smaller pro races – in Saint-Brieuc, Brittany. He had been tracked by Louviot for months and the meeting between the trio, as the Tour stopped in Tom's adopted French base, signalled a turning point in his promising career. Robinson's guiding hand during the talks was the first gesture of many that he would give to a rider who was to follow in his footsteps in Europe.

"Tom was a special case," Brian told me. "He was erratic, was fun to be with and I'm the opposite way; I'm dour and cautious. He was an extrovert. He had already made his name as an independent in France when he came to see us in the Tour. He said he wanted to turn pro and I introduced him to Louviot and he (Louviot) knew all about him straight away. The following year I picked him up from Harworth as a teammate."

Back then Robinson was coming to the end of a relatively short yet impressive career; he had ventured into the unknown and succeeded. It was just the start for Simpson. Tom was the youngest of six children, and was born in the village of Haswell, County Durham, in 1937. He was brought up in the working men's club that his family ran while his father, Tom senior, worked down the local coal mines during the Second World War. But lessening coal reserves forced the family to move down to Harworth as Tom senior sought more mining work, before he later found a job at a glass factory near the family's new home.

Soon enough Tom junior was racing around the village on an old butcher's bike, which he used to deliver meat for a local shop, and set his sights on upgrading it. His competitive nature didn't need encouraging. By the age of 13 he had followed his older brother Harry's lead by signing up as a member of the Harworth and District Cycling Club, and made it his mission to catch up with the older boys and find himself some new wheels. He was raised as a cyclist on the roads of South Yorkshire, Lincolnshire and Derbyshire, although he never really considered himself a Yorkshireman.

Tom would shelter in the air pocket behind the bigger, more senior riders, desperately hanging on to the back of the bunch during Sunday club runs to the Lincolnshire coast and on the moors neighbouring Sheffield. Through sheer perseverance he won the respect of his clubmates, even earning the nickname 'Four-Stone Coppi' – making light of his skinny physique with a nod to legendary Italian road racer Fausto Coppi. It was a tongue-in-cheek compliment he revelled in as images of Coppi – a charismatic rider known for winning continental clashes through glorious solo breakaways – adorned the teenager's bedroom walls growing up. It was European road racing that inspired him.

It was during those early outings that his uncompromising competitive streak flourished. A likeable, light-hearted joker off the bike would transform into a ruthless and fierce racer on it, particularly if anyone beat him. The frustration of defeat would drive him to push the limits to train and race even harder. His frail build began to develop after he started racing competitively as a 15-year-old in 1952 and soon enough he was winning regional time trial titles, while practically living on the bike.

But, like many who saw the bright lights of continental road racing in the magazines of the time, he yearned for the chance to give bunched racing a go. It prompted him to join Rotherham-based road club Scala Wheelers as the cycling civil war between the time trial traditionalists of the NCU and BLRC road race revolutionists continued. The drama and glory of those glossy, exotic publications fast made him a man on a mission to race like his heroes in Europe. For his early amateur races across the North of England, he even bought and raced in Italian national team jerseys that he had seen his hero Coppi wearing. He stood out like a sore thumb.

Confident in his ability and infatuated with the sport, Tom had his heart set on becoming a professional cyclist but knew he needed a back-up plan that would also fund his dream and pay into the family coffers. At 16 he started work as an apprentice draughtsman at a factory in Retford, North Nottinghamshire – cycling there and back every day, of course – while he studied the sport, collected books and magazines and even sent letters to the great and good of the sport asking for help and advice. He was determined to succeed. One of the men who responded to talented Tom in his pre-pro days was George Berger – an Austrian-born racer who spent years competing in France. Tom soaked up every piece of information, from saddle adjustments and equipment guidance to insights into the training and attitude of the continentals.

In a move aimed at improving Tom's cycling in the long-term, Berger urged the teenager to concentrate on track cycling and more specifically the individual pursuit – where riders start on opposite sides of the track and try to complete 4km faster than their opponent. It was thought it could help him build up his stamina and learn to sustain high speeds for long periods. The move from track to road is still a staple of the early careers of pros even today – a certain Sir Bradley Wiggins can vouch for that. Learning from experienced racers also saw him heed the words of former track star Cyril Cartwright regarding rigid race dieting and getting the right amounts of sleep.

Spurred on by the advice, Simpson, now 18, came second in the pursuit at the 1956 British National Championships after two punctures in the final led him to concede victory, despite having produced the fastest time ever recorded on Fallowfield's track in an earlier round. He then utilised that form to claim bronze in the team pursuit – where four riders race in each other's slipstream, rotating who rides on the front, while aiming to chase down an opposing four-man team over a 4km distance – on the track at the 1956 Olympic Games in Melbourne. He was a man possessed.

The following year he came second in the national 25-mile time trial championships and in 1958, after a bad track crash in Paris and then a stint track racing in Belgium, Tom decided to ramp up his pursuit of his ultimate goal: a career as a pro bike rider. He quite literally went back to the drawing board, working as a qualified draughtsman at the same Retford glass factory as his dad, labouring every hour available to give him the financial clout to have a real crack at breaking Europe. He persuaded a couple of French riders who were friends of a friend in Saint Brieuc to put him up, and arrived as a fresh-faced 21-year-old in 1959. Armed with nothing more than £100 and two racing bikes, it was now or never.

He'd entered a new world of racing but at this sink or swim junction, Tom's raw talent shone through. He began picking up prize money that was more than enough to sustain him and his exploits as a lone Englishman in France soon garnered publicity. The language barrier did prove an early obstacle however, as canny French amateurs quickly learned to use it to force misunderstandings and give Tom the slip.

He gained an independent licence, which practically made him a semi-pro rider, and the first sponsors got on board with a burgeoning talent who stood out from the crowd. His piercing smile and quick wit, teamed with an unforgiving yearn for glory, won admirers across the region. French lessons were the next step and he even met a Yorkshire woman, Helen Sherburn, a nanny working in Saint Brieuc, as he settled into life abroad like few of his compatriots had done before him.

From a cycling point of view, Tom got his first real taste of the picture-book races he aspired to during the Route de France – the same eight-stage marathon for top under 25s that bewildered Robinson years earlier. His European stage racing baptism led him up immense mountain passes like the mythical Tourmalet, the likes of which he'd never seen before, never mind cycled up. Yet he found that the mammoth Yorkshire club runs of his youth had at least given him some preparation for daily distances edging 200km.

He showed well during the race and before long was in that Brittany hotel with Raymond Louviot, the directeur sportif (team director) of the St Raphael team, negotiating a contract. His early days in the team were not an easy ride. He was plying his trade in a French team full of French riders hoping to maintain the status quo. Tom had to stand out and impress enough to become a senior pro.

Tom raced in his first World Championships in Holland that year. The Worlds road race – a one-day Classics-style race consisting of riders competing in national teams – is up there among the most coveted events on the cycling calendar. The winner gets to wear the prestigious rainbow jersey at every road race that follows for 12 months; a crown perhaps only topped by that of Tour de France yellow jersey winner. Typically, Tom was far from shy when it came to taking on the world's elite over a 290km course. In what would prove a trademark of the Simpson style, Tom went on the attack time after time during what was the longest single race he'd ever been involved in. He finished an impressive fourth behind established stars like Tour de France stage winner Andre Darrigade. It was a revelatory statement of intent.

Tom had shown he could mix it with the cream of the international cycling crop on any given day. He clearly had the pure speed to stay with and challenge the leaders during one-day Classics and his successful debut season finished in fitting style. He took part in the Baracchi Trophy – a two-man time trial in Italy – and competed against his cycling idol, the great Fausto Coppi. But tragically, Coppi, who won two Tours de France and five Giros, died within months after contracting a tropical disease aged just 40. It was in this race five years later that Tom would test himself to such an extent that he told one teammate he thought he was dying. It was an

Tom Simpson pictured after completing a race. (PA)

ominous sign that he was pushing his body to dangerous extremes.

The 1960 season saw Tom not-so-much come to the fore, but take centre stage. Paris-Roubaix is probably the most feared of all one-day bike races. Rightly considered a Monument for the sheer dread with which it fills riders, the race is among the sport's most historic. It features famous cobbled sections of road that the peloton has to somehow navigate usually in treacherous gales and rain. It is also among the most exciting and cringe-inducing spectacles in the sport to watch, with the danger of a massive pile-up never far away. The event is known in racing circles as the 'Hell of the North', and on a gusty, wet day it's not hard to see why. The 1960 edition was the first ever to be televised live, bringing cycling to a whole new audience of armchair viewers. One man stole the show – and that man was Tom Simpson.

His kamikaze breakaway tactics led him to dominate the hour of live TV screen time. He had raced away from the pack in a bid to get clear of the almost inevitable peloton implosion but was hunted down by the eventual winner Pino Cerami just before the finish, scraping in, exhausted, in ninth place.

But Tom was the hero, the brave loser, and his primetime showing sparked the start of a love affair with the continental media. Simpson played up to the clichéd image of the English gent, partly on the advice of his agent. He was pictured in magazines strolling the streets of Paris in a dapper suit topped off with a bowler hat and dubbed 'Major Simpson'. It was a nickname that stuck and a PR stunt that turned a working class miner's son into the embodiment of the Major Thompson character from the Pierre Daninos books of the 1950s. Major Thompson was a walking stereotype; a tall, dark and handsome English cavalry officer-turned-city slicker whose adventures told of witty comparisons between French and British society at the time. Tom was suddenly a celebrity and he didn't at all mind playing up to his new-found image. At the end of the day popularity equalled bigger contracts and access to sponsorship, and he was quickly becoming one of the faces of the sport.

Simpson's endearing personality and blossoming profile off the bike combined with his persona as a brave trailblazer on it. He would throw every last ounce of energy into races, often overdoing it, often crashing and usually getting back up and carrying on. He was relentless. His old teammate Brian Robinson summed it up perfectly. Smiling as he relived the 1960 Tour du Sud-Est, he said: "It was the second stage race of the season and Tom was going downhill and he had a horrible crash behind me. He got back up and I said 'Sit in my wheel, I will take you downhill'. Ten minutes later there's another bloody crash, and it was Tom. We got back to the bunch in the end and he won the race. He was special, Tom."

Robinson, recognising Tom's growing popularity and the lure of glitzy distractions, tried to guide his spontaneous teammate down the sensible route he had followed to obtain the rare privilege of European acceptance. But there was no stopping Tom, he was an impulsive man who lived life to the full. One well publicised illustration of Simpson's nature saw Brian, who had been advising Tom to look after his cash, arrive back at the Parisian apartment they shared with Elliott to find that his bright-eyed teammate had splashed out on an Aston Martin DB2 sports car. Tom Simpson had arrived. "He fitted in exactly," Brian told me. "He did everything he was supposed to do and things he wasn't supposed to do. He was that sort of guy."

His debut Tour de France later that year started with typical exuberance, and it came against the wishes of his boss Louviot. At just 22 – an age many considered too young to be able to complete the Tour – Tom was offered a place on the Great Britain team alongside elder statesman Robinson and he took it. He went hell for leather on the first few stages, placing fifth after the first day, before the gruelling three-week grind caught up with him. He miraculously finished the race in 29th place, arriving in Paris two stones in weight lighter and exhausted. But merely completing the world's hardest bike race was never going to be enough.

In 1961 Tom scored his first really historic victory; he won a treasured Monument, the Tour of Flanders. The pride of the Flemish people, this prestigious Belgian race put Tom in the history books. He launched two trademark attacks and was followed each time by Italian sprinter Nino de Filippis but Tom eventually outsmarted his opponent by pretending he was out of energy during the last circuit of the track on which they finished. He then summoned every last drop of energy to steam past, catching the Italian unaware, in a sprint to the line. He became the first Briton to win a Classic since 1896.

Tom's landmark win came as his old pal and mentor Robinson was going back to his roots. The lifestyle of a cyclist, living out of a suitcase away from his wife and young children, was becoming too much of a stretch and, in his early 30s, he had edged past his physical peak. It was time to go home; not to a cycling superstar's welcome, but to the building trade. "When I decided to finish I came back on the Saturday and started work on the Monday and nobody knew any different," he said.

Tom and Helen married and moved to Ghent for the 1962 season, reuniting them with a racing community he had been briefly introduced to years earlier. The fabled Tour de France, which was being contested by trade teams as opposed to national teams for the first time, was his main target and he gave it everything. Early on in the '62 race he scored some promising stage results before the first mountain route, stage 12, took in the Tourmalet, Aspin and Peyresourde peaks. The triple threat of Cols was not going to put him off though. Tom made his move in a battle against two of the greatest hill climbers in the history of the sport. Federico Bahamontes, known as the 'Eagle of Toledo', and Charly Gaul fought it out while Tom assessed the time gaps and made sure he rolled over the line to take the overall lead and become the first Brit to wear the Tour's 'Maillot Jaune' – the coveted yellow jersey. He was out in front in the world's most gruelling bike race; a feat it would take a full 32 years for one of his fellow countrymen to repeat.

The golden glory of racing in yellow may have been short-lived for Tom – due to a disappointing time trial the day after and a painful fall during a gung-ho mountain descent in a later stage – but he arrived in Paris in sixth place with his celebrity status enhanced yet further. The contracts rolled in and he collected his post-Tour rewards confident that winning the Tour de France was not an impossibility.

But in 1963 Tom began a long and bumpy relationship with his new team Peugeot. Over the coming years, the tumultuous partnership would leave him without a team car for support when he had mechanical issues at crucial stages in races and left him feeling that he didn't have the full support of the team. Regardless, Tom continued to pour himself into winning races.

Bordeaux-Paris was a relic of cycling's early super endurance races, taking on an unbelievable one-day distance that tested even the pros to their limits. It was last ridden by professionals in 1988 and it was Tom's first major triumph of 1963. The 365-mile marathon, which saw riders sit in the slipstreams of 'Derny' motorbikes for the final 180 miles, started at 2am and for Tom it finished 15 hours and 43 minutes later; well ahead of everyone else. Crowds lined the streets in their thousands as he rolled into the Parc des Princes stadium for a triumphant victory lap. He had won another Classic but, despite having the win in the bag, asked his pacer to speed up. Tom wanted to get the time for the fastest lap around the track – a move that could earn him some extra prize money – and he almost pulled it off. He had to win, he had to give everything he had. Simpson's ability and desire to go faster and further than anyone else, while crashing through the pain barrier, was a trait that was both admirable and dangerous in equal measure.

Tom's will to win drove him to victory in two more Monuments over the next two years. First he won Milan San-Remo, which is known to Italians as 'La Primavera', in 1964 by sprinting away from the Tour de France's nearly man Raymond Poulidor – he finished second three times and third five times but never won it outright. It took 45 years for another Brit to succeed in Milan-San Remo. Tom then went on to triumph in the Tour of Lombardy in 1965, adding to his growing array of Classics triumphs.

But it was a different victory in 1965 that secured his status as one of cycling's greats. Simpson led a strong British team including the likes of Vin Denson, Michael Wright, Alan Ramsbottom, Keith Butler and an up-and-coming Yorkshireman named Barry Hoban to San Sebastian, Spain, to contest the World Championship road race – another race that had never before given a Brit the privilege of wearing its iconic leader's jersey. Hoban, who grew up in Stanley, Wakefield, looked up to the elder statesman of the team. Simpson had become the yardstick for young riders aspiring to do great things in Europe.

Despite competition from superstars of the time, including feared German sprinter Rudi Altig, two-time Giro d'Italia winner Franco Balmamion and former World Champion Jean Stablinski, Tom's team worked relentlessly for him before he left them in pursuit of the win on what was a hilly route. He took Altig with him on a break from the pack and, with 1km to go on the last of 14 laps of a 19km course, Tom pulled out the sprint finish of his career, pounding the pedals until he had absolutely nothing left. Tom Simpson's moment had come and he powered to victory. He had earned a year in rainbow colours. He was Britain's first ever male road race World Champion; a World Champion who'd learned his trade on Yorkshire tarmac.

The real life Major Thompson's celebrity grew to heights previously thought inconceivable for a cyclist. Dubbed 'Mr Tom' by fans, he was the darling of the French and a conqueror of the continent to his growing army of fans in the UK. British Prime Minister Harold Wilson even presented the miner's-son-done-good with the Sportswriter's Personality of the Year prize, which was voted for by British journalists from all sports. Tom's trademark wit took over. He corrected the PM's assertion that he was a famous Yorkshireman, stating he was actually from Durham, and joked: "Mr Prime Minister, we are both in the saddle – you at Number 10 and me on my bike – but I hope your bottom doesn't hurt like mine does."

Tom transcended sport that year, also picking up the BBC Sport Personality of the Year Award. His feat of sporting achievement as a British cyclist and bike riding celebrity was for decades seen as a one-off. His beaming smile became the brave face of a sport of suffering, stamina and strength that had been heavily neglected back home as an unfathomable obsession of the people of continental Europe.

But, despite Tom's new-found hero status in Britain, his fortunes took a turn for the worse in 1966 before the season had even begun. He broke his leg while on a skiing trip and it hampered his preparation for the Tour de France he yearned to win so much. He threw himself back into training at the earliest possible opportunity and, when the race came around, he tried to fight his way into contention from the off. He stuck to his familiarly entertaining style, breaking from the peloton in pursuit of solo glory in energy-sapping moves during the early stages of the three-week marathon. But as the fatigue set in and the overall time gap to the leaders widened, the final days of racing became win or bust scenarios for Tom. He was in the running for wins on several stages – taking sixth on stage four, tenth places on eight and nine, and a ninth on stage 14 – but his luck ran out when he was forced to abandon during stage 17. He had been knocked from his bike by a press motorcycle during a mountainous descent the previous day as he tried desperately to distance himself from the race leader Julio Jimenez and make an assault on the podium places. It left him with a deep laceration to his right arm and, though he bravely battled on against the

Road Race World Champion Tom Simpson is handed his 1965 Sportsview Personality of the Year Award from Sir Stanley Rous at BBC Television Centre. (PA)

advice of his team doctor, he couldn't continue. At the start of stage 17 he could barely hold on to his own handlebars.

It was a setback that only served to intensify his desire to win a Tour de France and join the legends of the sport in the history books. The fact that the '67 Tour would be contested by national teams for the first time in six years fanned the flames of Tom's ambition. It would allow him to break free from the unpredictability of his splintered Peugeot team and go for victory backed by a band of albeit inexperienced riders that he could count on. At the age of 29 he was at his physical peak and he had years of elite experience behind him. He was determined that 1967 would be his year; it had to be.

By the time the great race came around, Tom had a plan. The 211km stage 13 was where he would make the move that would ultimately clinch him the yellow jersey. When the peloton reached the giant Mont Ventoux climb, he would strike and build an unassailable lead. A victory in the time trial later in the Tour might seal the win he craved so much. A couple of hiccups and a bout of stomach problems on the lead up to stage 13 only served

A display in Harworth featuring memorabilia from the career of Tom Simpson.
(Chris Lawton, YPN)

The memorial to Tom Simpson stands on the bleached mountainside of Mont Ventoux. (YPN)

to crystallise his ambition further. Tom needed to overhaul an eight-minute gap between him and the overall leader to take top spot.

He had suffered particularly on stage 10 over the 8,700ft Galibier mountain pass; meaning, in his mind, he needed to go for broke up the Ventoux. The climb itself is an unrelenting 21.5km ascent out of Bedoin in the Provence region of Southern France. The current record for climbing the last 15km is more than 48 minutes, putting its 'Giant of Provence' nickname into context. But there is something else about the Ventoux that makes it stand out from the Tour's other legendary Cols. It is a high altitude hell; a barren moonscape of limestone that glows in the summer heat, reflecting the sunlight to create a natural furnace.

As Tom reached the foot of the climb on July 13th 1967, temperatures at the summit had rocketed to a blistering 54C. Desperate to succeed, he stuck to the script and tried to execute his plan following a breakaway launched by top climbers Jiminez and the 'eternal second' Poulidor; but Tom was in no fit state.

He couldn't keep up the pace and began to slip back, all the while pushing his body further and further beyond its limits. With the summit in sight, he began weaving from one side of the road to the other in complete and utter exhaustion. His race mechanic Harry Hall rushed to his side and Tom apparently uttered the immortal words: "Put me back on my bike."

He somehow mustered more energy, now only 1.5km from the top of the peak, before he collapsed once again. Tom was unconscious and, despite the best efforts of medical staff, he could not be resuscitated. He died at the age of just 29 in his quest to win the Tour de France. A memorial stone now stands at the place on the mountain that his race and his life ended that day in 1967.

But the story of Tom Simpson was not over. His death raised serious questions about the Tour de France and how such a fit and well-respected athlete could die racing. A post mortem found that he had died of heart failure due to heat exhaustion, but traces of amphetamines and alcohol were also found in his system. This was a time when many riders had openly talked about the use of drugs in sport but a scandal involving the death of one of the world's most adored riders brought the issue to the top of the agenda. He was branded a cheat by some and a victim by others.

For his friend and former teammate Brian Robinson, Tom Simpson had unquestionable natural talent but an equally intense desire to win that led him down a dark path. "He went over the top at times and unfortunately he did that with drugs," Brian told me. "In those days Anquetil said 'I can't race without drugs' and a lot of people did it. We will never get rid of this problem by the look of it. It's the decision the man himself takes. It's your handlers. It's a big decision to say 'no'."

One thing is for sure, Tom was not alone. A murky undercurrent of drug taking has existed in cycling since the very first riders competed for cash in the late 1800s. From cocaine, alcohol and amphetamines to cortisone and EPO, substances have coursed through the veins of Grand Tour pelotons throughout history and in many ways Tom Simpson's death was symptomatic of a doping culture. He was no advocate of drug taking, in fact interviews with teammates and clips of him during the time suggest he had an uneasy relationship with the very idea of doping. He believed he was the best natural bike rider in the world and stimulants, perhaps in his own mind, had been justified as a means of levelling the playing field. Long before revered five-time Tour winner Anquetil famously said: "You can't ride the Tour de France on mineral water," Tom's childhood hero, the great Fausto Coppi, was asked whether he took "la bomba" – a mix of caffeine, cola and amphetamine pills. He replied: "Yes, whenever it is necessary." Then asked when it is necessary, he added: "Almost all the time."

We will never know how and why Tom made the decisions around doping that he did but the fact he is still so revered among the cycling community of the day and of the present tells a story in itself. This was a man who lived out his childhood dream of racing on the continent against the odds but whose experience was soured by the imperfections of the era. Tom was a character who had a deep-rooted love for the sport that blossomed in the hills of the White Rose and whose infectious desire spawned a similar passion for cycling in generations to follow. He simply went too far in his drive to succeed.

For Robinson, Simpson's demise is made far more upsetting when his natural potential is considered. "Tom had the ability to win without them (drugs) definitely and that's the sad bit," he told me. "All these guys were in the same boat. Anquetil had the talent without drugs, but one starts and the other says 'I need to beat him, so I'll take this'. Tom's fault was he had to win, he was over ambitious. It's good in a way but not something to die for."

Barry Hoban in action.

THE RELIABLE CAMPAIGNER

Cycling was in mourning. The extrovert entertainer Tom Simpson had died; the Tour had lost one of its favourite sons. Dutch rider Jan Janssen won stage 13 as the news of Tom's collapse and eventual death filtered through the crowd and riders.

The next day, as a mark of respect, the European riders decided not to contest the stage in order to pave the way for a British cyclist to take the victory. The man who would take the win in Tom's honour would be a West Yorkshire lad who had ambitions of his own. His name was Barry Hoban.

Amid the sorrow of losing one of the most liked and well-respected members of the peloton in Tom, the symbolic victory that his teammate and fellow Brit claimed was in many ways a fitting handover; although nobody, apart from Barry himself, really knew it at the time. Barry would be the next dominant British cyclist, pushing the envelope on his country's behalf for the decade to follow.

Tom and Barry were friendly but did not consider themselves close. They both had raw pace, they both loved cycling, they both came from working-class backgrounds and the pair of them were fierce competitors. But while Tom was the class clown, Barry was a straight-talker. In some ways they were poles apart yet their stories are forever intertwined. "We respected each other," Hoban told me. "Tom was very, very courageous; but I was as well."

Tom, two and a half years Barry's senior, both set the marker for what appeared achievable for a determined Northerner in Europe and impressed on his junior what it took to get to the top. Simpson's meteoric rise was the template for success that a generation prescribed to.

Born in February 1940, Barry grew up in West Yorkshire as one of five children. His father Paddy had served in the Second World War and worked all hours to feed and clothe his family during the post-war recovery effort. Stanley, a working-class industrial village on the Leeds-Wakefield border, became home to one of the country's very first council estates during Barry's youth and was an area where hard graft was simply a way of life. The community was centred around its coal mines and stone quarries.

His dad used to cycle on the track and road – even riding with Brian Robinson as a veteran during the 1940s – and his shed was an Aladdin's cave of old bike parts. It fascinated Barry, who cobbled together his first fixed gear bike from old spares including wooden wheels, a steel frame and green racing tubular tyres. It was a revelation to him and soon Barry and his bike were inseparable.

Even today, well into his late 70s, Hoban talks about those early days like they were yesterday. He vividly remembers waiting for his friends to pass his house on the school bus, before cycling behind on his patchwork bike and marking the back of it with his front tyre in a bid to show off to his pals. He then sprinted past, beating the bus to school. "Talk about street cred," he said. "I was king of the kop!"

Real racing first crossed his path during the area's regular sports days that were laid on for the families of Stanley's mining community. They would have grass track bike races and Barry needed no invitation.

By the age of 15 he had joined the Calder Clarion Cycling Club in Wakefield and his life changed forever. The Sunday club runs anchored his existence and became his focus at a time when life in Britain and in Yorkshire was far more solitary. Families stayed within the communities they knew, besides holiday breaks to the English coast. But Barry and his clubmates would regularly saddle up and ride 75 miles to places like Scarborough for the day and then ride home for a bit of fun on a weekend. His aptitude for cycling and his sense of adventure proved the ticket to a world outside his home village.

"We were 16 and 17 and we didn't think that was training, but it was," he told me. "You almost lived on the bike. I used to ride out to a race in, for example, Ilkley 30 miles away. Then I'd ride the race that was maybe 60 miles and ride home; and that's 120 miles altogether. All that accumulated up and that strength I'd built up when I got to the continent meant I wasn't afraid of the distances. I was a bit hard as nails."

The familiar story of in-fighting between the time trial and the road racing communities was also a factor in Barry's development. His Calder club was firmly NCU, focusing on time trials, and he initially saw road racing as a bit of a distant dream anyway. In those days as an unproven amateur you would need a bike with gears – an expensive luxury at the time that limited many young upstarts to time trials – to be able to road race. Seeing the 1954 Tour of Britain pass by his house further whetted his appetite.

Seasoned by club runs and relishing his time on the bike, Barry started an apprenticeship as an electrician down the mines and began saving for those elusive hill-conquering gears. In 1957, aged 17, he was finally in a position to test himself in the bunch races he had read about.

Former rider and professional Yorkshireman Ron Kitching planted the road racing seed for young Hoban and many of his contemporaries. Kitching owned and operated one of the most successful bicycle, parts and kit importing businesses in the UK from the 1940s onwards. It would release 'Everything Cycling' catalogues that were considered kit bibles for aspiring pros, and ran a cycling emporium in Harrogate town centre. Discovering Ron Kitching's treasure trove of a shop opened Barry's eyes to the world of road racing on the continent; the top floor was bedecked with glossy European cycling magazines and an array of pristine jerseys adorned with the names of legends like three-time Tour de France winner Louison Bobet.

Eyes firmly fixed on the prize of Europe, Barry invested in continental-style road jerseys and some white cloth to make Calder Clarion appear more professional. He even enlisted the stitching skills of his mum to plaster the words Clarion on the front panels. He began taking part in the circuit-based British road races of the time and discovered what he calls the "magic" of going head-to-head with fellow riders in bunched finales; scenarios that unearthed his lethal sprint finishes.

The legends of the European scene seemed like they were a world away from West Yorkshire but products of God's Own Country were making inroads on the continent. As a youth Barry was aware of Brian Robinson's feats but it was Tom Simpson who proved his real inspiration. Tom was taking the steps Barry wanted to take in advance of him, and made his goals seem achievable. Simpson was dominating his final amateur meet on the Fallowfield track in Manchester, with Barry wistfully looking on, when the penny dropped that the pacey Stanley rider had a chance. Hoban told me: "He (Simpson) was the person who really inspired me and he was two and a half years ahead of me and as a youngster, two and a half years is an age."

The assertion that the pair were inseparable friends does not sit well with Barry. They would later be teammates, rivals and Barry would go on to help bring up Tom's children after marrying his widow Helen. But no matter what their relationship became, Barry looked up to Tom during his early years as a racer. "As I saw Tom progressing I thought we were very similar in many aspects," he remembered. "We could both ride a very, very good time trial and both ride long distance to the Dales very well and were good on the track: I was twice national pursuit champion. Suddenly I thought 'if Tom Simpson can do it, I can too, everything he's done I've done'. Tom was a real inspiration."

He saw Tom fly the nest to race as an independent in France in 1959, before winning the admiration of big pro team bosses and following in Brian Robinson's footsteps by signing with St Raphael-Geminiani. Seeing the

Barry Hoban wins stage eight of the 1975 Tour de France in Bordeaux.

blueprint had inspired Hoban further to formulate his own plan to break into continental road racing.

Like Robinson, he was meticulous and calculated; focussed in the pursuit of success. He set about saving up some money and following Simpson's lead by eventually taking the leap of faith to France as an independent and racing in amateur and smaller pro races in the hope of being spotted by a pro outfit. Saving to sustain a fledgling career as a full-time cyclist was the first major part of the battle. It would provide the cash that allowed a young rider time to adapt without the immediate need to start bringing home prize money; it was a short-term safety blanket.

In between working down the mines and training, Hoban spotted another opportunity to further himself. He again followed Simpson's lead by securing a place in a GB Olympic team pursuit track cycling squad. And although the 1960 Rome Games did not present him with silverware, he gained invaluable experience on the international stage. It was all part of the plan. In all it took him three years to scrape together the £200 he needed to give himself a chance to road race abroad, and in 1962 he made his way across the Channel unsure of what to expect.

In reality what awaited bright-eyed Barry was an ultra-competitive infrastructure of riders and events that had developed over decades of honing the practice of road racing. It meant tougher races, longer distances, higher mountains and being the focus of attention in towns and villages that lived and breathed the sport. Even getting used to the idea that roads would be closed during races – so you didn't have to stick to one side of the road to avoid traffic during cornering – illustrated the chasm in cycle racing culture.

"In those days the Channel might as well have been 3,000-miles wide because of the difference it meant between British cyclists and continental cyclists," he explained. "It could have been the Atlantic Ocean."

On top of adjusting to the racing norms, Barry, then 22, had to adapt to the language and gain his 'road legs' after spending the previous winter track cycling in South Africa. He moved to Arras in Northern France after gaining a small contract with a local club that was sponsored by the Bertin cycling company, which had links with Ron Kitching back in Yorkshire. The different tastes in food and the language barrier could have turned Hoban's dream into dust but, like Robinson and Simpson before him, he stuck with it. "I couldn't speak a word of French but if nobody can speak English to you it's sink or swim," he told me. "I can only remember a couple of weeks when I couldn't get understood. You've got to cotton on pretty quick. It wasn't easy; don't think I didn't think at times in my small hotel, 'what the bloody hell am I doing here with no family or home life?'"

Beating up-and-coming local hopefuls on their own patch didn't go down well either. Neither European road racing fans, residents or local race organisers wanted to see a Brit take home their prize money. It was by no means an easy ride. But his time as "public enemy number one" was short-lived and, upon settling into the speed of life in France and learning at least the lingo he needed to work his way through the peloton, he became one of the British brigade that earned the respect and adoration of the people there. Soon the bond between the locals and their adopted rider matured, and as he rode through the country lanes of Northern France screams of 'vas-y-Barry!' – French for 'go on Barry' – quickly became the norm. And for Hoban, there was an unusual familiarity about life in Arras.

"The working area produces a character of people and Yorkshire has always been a big working class area; the steelworks, mills and factories," he said. "There was a lot of hard work and people knuckled down and did it; they weren't afraid to work and go on and do it. The working environment creates the people completely. I left an industrial coal mining area of West Yorkshire and went to Northern France, which was an industrial coal mining, working class area and the mentality was exactly the same; the only difference was they spoke a different language. They were the salt of the earth."

It was that mirrored attitude towards the sport and hard graft in general that stuck with Barry; and it had to.

He signed for the Mercier Hutchinson BP pro team in 1964 after winning 36 races – and finishing sixth in the new Tour de France for independents, the Tour de l'Avenir, in 1963 – in his first two years in France. The pro lifestyle he walked into was incredibly tough. Through training and racing riders were expected to cycle up to 30,000 miles a year over some of the most imposing and fear-inducing hills in the world. His role was to support team leader Raymond Poulidor – or 'Pou Pou' as he was rather unfortunately nicknamed.

Looking back, 1964 was a stunning debut year for the Yorkshireman. The young neo-pro claimed two stages of the Vuelta a España – becoming the first Brit to win a Spanish Tour stage – and was arguably robbed of his first Tour de France stage win after being manhandled in a sprint finish with Jan Graczyk. But his success didn't stop him returning to Stanley and selling European jerseys to his mates in West Yorkshire to get him through the winter each year.

His rapid rise didn't go unnoticed by the top pro teams and riders, including Tom Simpson. Barry still talks of the time when, as a young upstart, he made a break from the peloton in which the senior British pro, Tom, was well placed. Tom promptly ordered his established friends in the pack to chase Barry down before telling him: "I'm the number one British rider on the continent, not you."

Within his team, Barry also played second fiddle to Mercier's star man Poulidor and felt he was often unfairly overlooked by his team manager, Antonin Magne, who only had eyes for the 'eternal second'. Like his British predecessors, he was finding it tough to conquer his trade team's French hierarchy. It was the Tour de France's temporary return to the national team format in 1967 that gave him his chance to shine.

He rode alongside his compatriot and career marker Simpson that year. But Tom's tragic death meant he had to take over the role as leader of the British team, painfully reassess and play a part in writing the next chapter. The gift of his victory in the '67 Tour in Tom's honour – fellow teammate and close friend to Tom, Vin Denson, has always said he, not

Hoban, was supposed to have been gifted the win by the peloton – marked a true fork in the road for British road racing in Europe. Barry would soon be leading a lone charge.

By 1968 he had moved to Tom's old stomping ground of Ghent, in Belgium, and was ready to lead Britain in the last Tour de France to be contested by national teams. In a sign of what was to come, he marked his debut Tour as leader with a new first; and this time it was far from a gift. His stunning win on stage 19 from Grenoble to Sallanches-Cordon – finishing with a four-minute lead after breaking away with 75 miles of Alpine riding still to go – was the first time a British rider had ever won a Tour de France mountain stage. To mark his victory, he was, of all things, awarded a cow called Estele for his hard work.

His tenure at the top of British cycling continued the next year with a third place in a Monument, Liege-Bastogne-Liege, which was won by the great Eddy Merckx. The young Belgian would go on to become the most lauded cyclist of all time, winning five Tours, five Giros, a Vuelta and every one-day Monument in the sport. Barry's ability to mix it with the likes of Merckx shows just how talented he was.

A shift back to trade teams from national teams by the organisers of the Tour de France initially helped Hoban. He became the first Brit to win two Tour stages back to back when he claimed stages 18 and 19 during the 1969 race. But the move also limited the opportunities available to his young compatriots. Only three Brits – Barry, Michael Wright and Derek Harrison – would make Tour trade teams that year. Many riders had either failed to make the grade, struggled to make ends meet, headed to domestic teams or had simply lost their passion for the sport after Tom's untimely death.

Barry rode on regardless and by 1970, as the perceived gap between British and continental cycling grew once more, he was the only Brit to take part in the Tour de France. During five of the 10 Tours de France during the 1970s Barry would be our nation's sole rider and when he missed the '76 event there were none at all. After the halcyon days of Simpson, British cycling was experiencing an extended lull abroad.

But as the British presence waned, Hoban's presence within the pro peloton grew. He was nicknamed the 'Grey Fox' as he matured into a grey-haired old hand, known for his masterful tactics and understanding of how to play the peloton. He was also meticulous in his pre-race planning, perfecting a detailed routine that would give him the best opportunity of the win; from painstakingly shaving his legs to knowing the intricacies of every race route. Such preparation helped him secure a famous podium in the gruelling Paris-

Roubaix race in 1972, before he beat Merckx to the prestigious Ghent-Wevelgem spring Classic in 1974.

Yet Barry's glory days came at a time when cycling's mainstream popularity in his homeland had suffered from a lack of British interest in big races and the hangover from Tom Simpson's tragic death. With that said, the Tour de France's bizarre first visit to Great Britain in 1974 could not have been timed any worse. It was not cycling demand or a desire to grow the sport in Britain that brought the world's top road racers here; it was artichokes. Believe it or not, produce growers in Brittany were credited with the idea of a British Tour stage as a way of marketing their vegetables to a new audience and publicising a newly opened ferry route to Plymouth, where stage two of the 1974 race would take place.

It was the route of the race itself that stayed long in the memories of cycling fans for all the wrong reasons. Riders were tasked with touring an immeasurably dull 7.5-mile circuit of the newly opened A38 bypass 14 times; and it didn't go down well with anyone. Relatively few cycling fans turned out to see what was going on and the lack of atmosphere and vanilla racing etched the stage in Tour folklore as a disaster. In fact, Barry Hoban – one of only two British competitors in the '74 Tour – declared the stage the most boring he'd ever ridden. Suffice it to say, the great race would not be back any time soon.

The last of Hoban's eight Tour stage victories came in 1975 – only one Brit, Mark Cavendish, has won more – in a career that saw the boy from Stanley race against some of the all-time greats and occasionally come out on top. When I asked him about those greats, his response – clearly fine-tuned over the years – is uttered with a reminiscent smile: "When I was 17, 18 and 19 I had three heroes. In the time trial I was Jacques Anquetil, up Holme Moss I was the Eagle of Toledo, Bahamontes, and in road races I was Rik Van Looy. These were my teenage heroes and little did I realise I would get to pit my wits and strength against them man to man. But the greatest was Eddy Merckx without doubt. No rider will ever do what Eddy Merckx did."

Barry's 12th and final Tour de France came in 1978 at the ripe old age of 38. And as the next generation of young British pretenders began making their way to Europe – many finding the continent less than welcoming – pro racing at home was growing in stature. It was catering to the needs of an increasing number of young riders who had grown up hearing about Simpson and Hoban when the bridge they built to Europe had long since eroded. Few would succeed in establishing themselves abroad.

"Unfortunately it was a big sacrifice to make to risk everything on the

Barry Hoban climbs up Kidstones Pass in the Yorkshire Dales. June 3 2013. (Bruce Rollinson, YPN)

continent and by then, in the '70s, we had a little pro scene in Britain," Barry told me. "A lot of riders preferred to be top of a small pool rather than bottom of a big one. It wasn't easy to do it and you had to do it yourself."

A year after finishing his last Tour, the Stanley veteran took part in the 260-mile Empire Stores London to Bradford Marathon race. Barry arrived in Bradford's Odsal stadium almost seven minutes ahead of his nearest rivals. It proved a fitting end to his career round-trip, from humble Yorkshire to the glamour of the continent and back again.

Fast forward a few decades and Barry still has that fire in his belly; you can tell. Reliving the moments that catapulted him into the pro peloton through telling his stories of life on the bike clearly stirs the blood even more than 35 years after his retirement. He still lives and breathes the sport.

Beryl Burton (YPN)

THE QUEEN OF THE ROAD

Yorkshire was no doubt the breeding ground for Britain's early success on the road. The county's stunning vistas and challenging hills seemed to combine with a work ethic drilled into a generation of youths in a post-war North tasked with rebuilding Britain.

Cycling struck a chord with a group of early pioneers who refused to take no for an answer when the world of continental racing appeared out of reach. Robinson overcame barriers of culture and language, Simpson charmed his way into European hearts with his ability and personality, and Hoban breached the Channel with unerring consistency and guile. Beryl Charnock, on the other hand, had a different set of challenges and was not brought up with the same innate passion for two wheels.

Born in Halton, Leeds, in 1937, Beryl grew up during hard times. Her home city was still a significant industrial force – it had been famed as a rail hub and for its mills and factories during the industrial revolution – but was in the grips of the Great Depression.

She was born to a mother who was a housekeeper and father who drove coaches for a living, and was raised amid the outbreak of the Second World War when Leeds became a centre for producing munitions. Rationing further impoverished a region battered by the Blitz in the early 1940s and life was a struggle as stories of war-time death and destruction filtered back home.

After the conflict, Beryl's family scraped by to raise her, her brother and sister in their adopted home in the Morley area of Leeds. But as a youngster, Beryl was different. She was a force of nature more or less from day one. She had a deeply ingrained competitive streak; always striving to outdo others and, more often than not, herself. She was never satisfied with second place. But she had cultural obstacles to overcome if she was to break the mould and translate her competitive nature into anything more than a hobby. She arrived in an utterly patriarchal period of British society; the men went out to work, while the women were housewives who raised the children. "That Yorkshire grit must have been born into her," her daughter Denise Burton-Cole told me. "She just liked to win and be the best."

At the age of 15 Beryl was determined to forge her own path in life after leaving school. Having talked her way into an administration job at the Sir Montague Burton high street clothing chain, she was introduced to the world of two wheels by a friendly co-worker, and cycling nut, named Charlie

Burton. It was love at first sight in more ways than one, but getting involved in Charlie's sport would have to be against doctor's orders.

As a child she had contracted rheumatic fever, a disease of the nervous system that can damage the heart. It interrupted her schooling as she spent nine months in hospital and a further year in recovery, before she was advised in her early teens to permanently steer clear of strenuous exercise. But that wasn't going to stop her – instead it was practically forgotten. Denise explained: "It was never spoken about. She just got on with it and what she wanted to do. We didn't know there was a problem at all until I was quite a young lady. Things like that weren't talked about; you didn't talk about the potential of that being disastrous."

By 1954, at the age of 17, Beryl became a member of the Morley Road Club and her growing infatuation with cycling and whirlwind romance with Charlie saw her married; becoming Beryl Burton a year later. Unsurprisingly, the couple enjoyed a honeymoon in their saddles on Yorkshire's east coast as cycling became their prime focus.

The Yorkshire Dales became her training ground; the region's landscape and country roads spurring her on just as they were doing for Simpson, Robinson and Hoban. The chance discovery of the bike proved the perfect outlet for her driven nature. Within three years of joining the Morley club, she was riding away from the fastest men on group rides and challenging preconceptions at a time when competitive female cyclists in Britain were few and far between.

But it did not take long for her natural ability to get due credit; this was no ordinary cyclist. "Most men appreciated what she was because the results were there," Denise told me. "There was no doubting how good she was and the men she beat; they really appreciated her. I don't think there was a barrier there; not in the cycling community anyway."

Beryl fell pregnant in 1955 but refused to let that get in the way of her passion for sport. Incredibly, she continued riding her bike until she was six months pregnant; adjusting her saddle and handlebars to accommodate her ever-growing bump along the way. Denise was born in January 1956. For a second time Beryl was told to avoid demanding exercise, this time

after doctors found she had an irregular heartbeat. The strong-minded Morley mum took the advice with a pinch of salt, of course.

For most women of the time, the birth of their first child would have heralded the start of a path towards domestic obscurity; the stereotypical mother hen dedicated to supporting others. But Beryl Burton was not 'most women'. Her husband had gone from cajoling partner to the all-in-one soigneur – a French cycling term for support staff who do everything from food preparation to massages. To his great credit, Charlie, in a period of staunch traditionalism, parked his own cycling ambitions, to support his incredibly gifted wife's ascent. Their home life was also far from typical. "My mum used to delegate the jobs," Denise said. "There was no way she would do them all herself. She did what she needed to do and that was quite something in those days. My dad just realised that my mum was a lot better than what he was and supported her absolutely. He drove her, as she never learned to. And he enjoyed it; that's what he wanted to do."

But living off a sole wage, having a scientific training plan or dedicating every aspect of their lives to cycling success was never a possibility for the Burtons. The prize money and prestige associated with the women's side of the sport during the 1950s was simply non-existent. Female cyclists were in it for the love of the sport and nothing else. Denise, who went on to win a World Championship bronze medal herself in the individual pursuit on the track in 1975, remembers those early days vividly: "It was difficult. All your spare money went on travelling and equipment. Just as I was, she was cycling to her events and hanging her racing wheels and any tools on her bike on the way. You had to fit your life in and around it."

Beryl was soon entering national competitions; taking on Britain's best for the first time in the 1957 season while working as a labourer in Yorkshire's famed 'Rhubarb Triangle' – an area that encompasses Barry Hoban's home village of Stanley – between Leeds and Wakefield. It was another male-dominated environment in which she thrived and challenged preconceptions. Far from cursing her job, she credited her work on a farm operated by fellow cyclist Norman 'Nim' Carline as a means of boosting her strength, while being flexible enough for her to keep on top of training.

Outside work she would be out testing herself on the Yorkshire hills she had fallen in love with. Rides lasting 100 miles added to her boundless strength. "She liked to go into the Yorkshire Dales, up Kettlewell and over the tops," Denise told me. "If she had a day she would do massive loops right through them; over any Dale I suppose. For a woman to go up to the Dales and over Buttertubs; that's pretty tough stuff. And in those days the women's races wouldn't have been as hard as that, so she's getting her strength, stamina and core strength from that hard training. She would just go out and do it. It certainly helped her."

As Brian Robinson experienced before her, British cycling during the 1950s largely centred around time trialling and the women's calendar focused on the British National Championships and the annual World Championships – female cyclists were not recognised by the Tour de France or Olympic Games until 1984.

The most coveted prize on the domestic cycling scene was the Best British All Rounder crown, which was won by the rider who recorded the best average speed on time trials covering 25, 50 and 100 miles during the calendar year. In her debut year on the scene – just a year after giving birth – Beryl ranked fifth.

She claimed her first national title, winning the 25-mile British time trial title the following year and made cycling history in 1959 by becoming the first female British World Champion in the 3,000-metre individual pursuit on the track; the first of five world track triumphs.

Yet Beryl's standout achievements were arguably her two world title wins in 1960 and 1967, becoming the first Briton to wear the coveted rainbow jersey in the domain of the continentals: the road. And she was a keen admirer of male road legends like Coppi; making such victories all the sweeter. In fact, at the 1960 World Championships in East Germany she was crowned double World Champion after also winning the individual pursuit in front of 60,000 people. On the continent she had become a celebrity, she was the world's greatest female cyclist. But at home she was virtually unknown; so much so that she once wrote that she might as well have won the ladies' darts final at the local pub for all the British public knew. Denise explained: "It wasn't something the newspapers or TV understood. You might get a mention but people weren't educated about it. If it happened now it would be so different."

Nevertheless, Beryl Burton broke countless world records, won seven world titles and an unbelievable 25 consecutive British Best All Rounder titles during a career unlikely ever to be replicated. She clearly did not ride for the fame and fortune, but for the love of the bike and the rush of victory. In fact, in many ways she was the opposite of what you might expect of an international sportsperson. At home at least, she was at times unfathomable. "In our house she was quiet, she was quite serious. In fact, not a lot was said unless it needed to be said," Denise remembered. "We didn't have a discussion or play a game. Some people would say it was quite Victorian how she brought us up. She was very, very different to what people write."

Perhaps her most famous moment came during the Otley Cycling Club 12-hour race on September 17th 1967. Setting off two minutes behind the male riders in the event, in which riders aimed to cover the biggest distance in the allotted time, Beryl stunned the field by catching the men's race leader Mike McNamara and offering him a Liquorice Allsort on the way past. She beat McNamara by three quarters of a mile, riding 277.25 miles, breaking both the men's and women's world record. It took male riders two years to surpass Beryl's marker, while the women's record still stands 50 years on despite the development of skinsuits, disc wheels and carbon fibre.

She also raced alongside and against Denise on several occasions, once even refusing to shake her daughter's hand after losing a sprint finish. She claimed Denise had not done her fair share of the work in maintaining a breakaway, but the pair soon made up. The Burton household was always a competitive environment. On one occasion Beryl ventured out for a training ride and, intrigued, Denise asked where she was going. York was the answer. "I followed her 15 minutes later as I thought 'I'm going to do a training ride too'," she said. "It ended up that she (Beryl) was coming down

Denise Burton-Cole, daughter of Beryl Burton, pictured with memorabilia at her home near Ripon. April 18 2014.
(Tony Johnson, YPN)

one side of the A64 and I was riding down the other and we waved at each other. It was funny really."

Her steely determination and will to win has become the stuff of legend. Not one to dwell on past successes, it seems Beryl's ability to push her body to the limit for decade upon decade ultimately proved her downfall. On May 5th 1996, while delivering invites to her 59th birthday party – on her bike, of course – she collapsed and died of heart failure on the very same roads that helped to shape her cycling story.

Beryl was not known for reflecting on the past, often keeping her thoughts to herself. Even Denise claims not to have been party to her mother's reminiscing. Beryl was somewhat of an enigma. She had obvious natural talent but her incomparable drive stood her and many of her male contemporaries apart.

"I think the bottom line is these people loved what they were doing and they knew and learned what it takes to get to the top and you don't let anybody get in your way to do it," Denise added. "That can make them feel harsh sometimes but at the top of the list was cycling. You had to be tough, you had to survive."

Within cycling circles Beryl Burton is a legend, having dominated her sport for decades in an understated and almost romantic fashion. She was awarded an OBE and a degree of national acclaim during her lifetime. Yet the down-to-earth housewife, labourer, keen gardener and mother only truly won the acclaim she deserved after her untimely death. The esteem with which her career was held by people in continental Europe and beyond was illustrated by the fact that donations to the Beryl Burton memorial fund were received from all over the globe – from Germany and Australia to Canada and the USA – after her death.

FAVOURITE TRAINING RIDES

"She (Beryl) liked to go into the Yorkshire Dales up Kettlewell and over the tops. If she had a day she would do massive loops right through them, over any Dale I suppose. She would go out for whole days at a time."

Beryl Burton, *according to Denise Burton-Cole*

Her decades of dominance in women's bike racing did not spark a mass surge in British female riders; it would be 15 years before we had another road World Champion, and even longer before women began to get the credit they deserved for their achievements. But we should never forget that Beryl Burton set the wheels in motion.

ANGUISH AND AMBITION

Men's road racing at home was taking on a life of its own and the European scene was quite simply moving on as Barry Hoban continued his lone mission abroad in the early 1970s.

The questions that Tom Simpson's death had posed around the use of drugs in the sport were not welcomed by the European cycling establishment. The sport's reputation had been damaged in Britain and in Europe, and it had a knock-on effect on the prospects of aspiring British pros.

Before his death Tom recognised the need to help riders make the transition to Europe and opened a hostel for cyclists with his long-time friend Albert Beurick in Ghent, Belgium. He also publicly called for a British-sponsored trade team of British riders that could beat the continentals at their own game; an ambitious but arguably achievable aim with a man like Tom at the helm. But without the plan's influential figurehead, the symbolic drawbridge across the Channel had been raised. Few Brits, never mind Yorkshiremen, would find their way over to cycling's mainland to achieve their far flung goals in the forthcoming decades. The tide had turned against a British success story.

Despite the climate, naked British ambition was still very much ever present. Raleigh industries had bought Carlton Cycles during the late 1960s. It came after bike manufacturer Carlton had provided bikes and sponsorship for British road racing teams in pro races on home turf and by 1971 it had stepped up its goals by eyeing success abroad. The British racing outfit that became known as TI Carlton was eventually rebranded as TI Raleigh and the project to achieve European success became seen as a means of boosting awareness and sales of the firm's bikes in different countries. It was a bold idea and one that echoed brave British endeavours of the past and near future in that it wasn't backed up by the experience or funds necessary to make it work. Initially, rather than setting up a base in Europe so the team could train on the hills they were due to race on, riders were shipped to Belgium or France for big events and then expected to return home to the UK the same day; it was nonsensical.

Raleigh eventually agreed to put their hands in their pockets and hired a more experienced team manager in the ultimate aim of winning the Tour de France. Successful ex-racer Peter Post – a stern Dutchman who had made his name as a rider winning Paris-Roubaix and track endurance events called 'Six-Days' – was appointed for the 1974 season and took the entire operation to Europe. His mix of British and Dutch pros would train in and engage with the continent, living under his arcane rule.

Middlesbrough-born sprinter Sid Barras was among the big British prospects snapped up by TI Raleigh. Like many of his contemporaries, Sid grew up idolising the first real road cycling celebrity to come out of his home country; Tom Simpson. In fact, he had a poster of Mr Tom on his wall growing up. Simpson embodied the Northern-boy-done-good dream that he aspired to and added to the mystique of cycling.

And the sport was in his blood. His dad, a fitter for a building firm, had been a keen pre-war time trial rider in his youth, racing in the days of codenamed venues and covert black uniforms to evade the police.

From an early age it was quite clear that Barras had the cycling bug. During our conversations he remembered the time he escaped as a toddler from his boyhood home in Teeside on a tricycle, before his dad found him pootling along to Redcar a few miles away. By his 10th birthday, Sid had been down to Bill Beattie's bike shop in Middlesbrough to collect his first bike and began time trialling as a schoolboy, rising through the ranks in the early 1960s with his natural turn of speed evident from the start. "A lot of the racing was in the North East to Newcastle and my dad would get six, seven or eight of us in the back of his builder's van, and sometimes we'd go as far down as Nottingham. Those were great times," he told me.

By the age of 14 he was heading out on 120-mile club runs and still vividly remembers climbing Dales ascents like Buttertubs Pass as a youngster on the same natural training grounds as Yorkshire's legends before him. He followed every Simpson race and held his hero up on a pedestal in the hope that one day he might even race alongside him. In 1967, with 19-year-old Barras rapidly progressing up the racing ladder at home, that distant dream was stolen away from him. It was only a year after Simpson's demise that Barras, who was training to be an electrician, made his breakthrough against the country's best amateurs by winning two stages and finishing fifth overall in the 1968 Milk Race – a prestigious multi-stage predecessor to the Tour of Britain – before narrowly missing out on a place at the Olympic Games in Mexico the same year. His ability to win road race bunch sprints was already starting to show.

But Simpson's death left a scar on Barras and the drugs question raised serious doubts in his own mind about whether he wanted to emulate his idol's move to the continent. In 1970 a small British outfit called Bantel made him a good offer to stay at home and compete on the national road racing circuit, which was slowly building, but by 1973 he was testing himself in Switzerland after his team received an invite to the Tour de Suisse (Tour of

Sid Barras (left) and Keith Lambert in action in 1979. (YPN)

Keith Lambert racing with teammate Sid Barras (right) in 1978. (YPN)

Switzerland). It was a punishing and prestigious nine-day Alpine stage race, which had been twice won by Fausto Coppi's great rival Gino Bartali in the 1940s. Barras' European bow went incredibly well given that the scale of the race was several levels up from the standard of racing at home. He won the first road stage, beating the great Classics winner Francesco Moser, and wore the leader's yellow jersey and green points jersey on consecutive days. What a start.

Boro-born Barras had arrived and was quickly drafted into the Anglo-Dutch TI Raleigh experiment but his unhappy time there ultimately killed off his desire to ride abroad. He was one of several British riders sold the Raleigh dream who left the team largely due to Peter Post in what proved a symbolic fork in the road for British cyclists. It was a sign of the re-emergence in some quarters of the kind of stigma and preconception about British riders that made Brian Robinson's career so impressive in the circumstances. Barras and the likes of Phil Bayton, who would go on to be a top domestic pro, feel they were forced out.

"I didn't get on with Peter Post," Barras told me. "Post basically wanted a Dutch team. I remember finishing fourth in the GP of Nice I think, I won the bunch sprint and I was really pleased and turned round and said to him 'I won the sprint' and he shrugged and said 'you didn't win'; and that was the treatment you got. He'd have the mechanic put training wheels on your bike and lighter racing wheels on for the others. It didn't last and there were other things I didn't want to do."

Post's perceived lack of support for the British contingent once led the team's six Britons to drive a van to the Het Volk Belgian one-day race from their training camp in Southern France while Post apparently gave his Dutch riders plane tickets. Post remained adamant until his death in 2011 that he had no prejudice against his Brits but the fact that his TI Raleigh team – consisting of nine Dutch riders and one Belgian – eventually won the Tour de France in 1980 through Joop Zoetemelk suggests he at least had a preference.

The "other things" Barras eluded to relate to the culture of doping he came across in Europe at the time; something that both surprised him and made his mind up on a return home to Yorkshire. It echoed of the same insidious problem that led to the death of Simpson just seven years earlier and his desire to ride 'clean' – without taking banned substances – brought him back to settle with his wife Linda in Laycock near Keighley. What he saw on the continent left an impact and coloured his view of Simpson even further.

"It broke down the myths for me," he said. "It was the culture of the sport. I don't judge anyone but I think Tom would have been the greatest anyway. If he were racing today, he would be number one. They reckon he could ride himself into the ground anyway. He was my hero. If he had still been alive three years later, I would have raced him – that's the sad thing."

An offer from his old team Bantel brought Barras back home and, in the time he'd been away, the British professional cycling scene had started to boom. He was winning an average of 18 races a season and was on good money; in his mind backing up his decision to return as he was "better off being number one in Britain than an also-ran for TI Raleigh". Yorkshire's roads became his training ground once again and he blossomed in domestic racing alongside the likes of Shipley's Dudley Hayton and Bingley's Keith Lambert, who won the national road race championship in 1974 and 1980.

Post, meanwhile, continued to implement his authoritarian style on his Raleigh setup while bringing in a new team ethos. He believed in not having a designated team leader so that they did not have to rely on one man. Every rider had the opportunity to win stages and his groups were notoriously well drilled. His Raleigh teams were unbeatable in the Tour de France's time trial stages from 1976 to 1982. Post did get results but the means by which he succeeded were unpopular to say the least. Under him, one by one ambitious British pros returned to the UK utterly disenchanted with the continental mindset. Post's apparent attitude towards the Brits was an illustration of the wider difficulties our riders were facing.

Only Barry Hoban's continued presence on the continental circuit kept the dream alive for young road racers aspiring to emulate the Tour's greats. But the enduring legacies of Yorkshire's cycling pioneers still fostered ambition in the next generation. Five years on, a new group of English-speaking riders were aiming to cross the Channel and give European racing a go themselves. In the late 1970s and early '80s the likes of Paul Sherwen, Graham Jones, Irish eventual Tour winner Stephen Roche and flying Scotsman Robert Millar would try to follow in the footsteps of Barry Hoban, who was still a staple part of the peloton. It was part of a movement dubbed as that of the 'Foreign Legion' thanks to the celebrated 1993 Rupert Guinness book of the same name.

They encapsulated a new generation enthused by the idea of cycling abroad. Their optimism and desire to race on the continent was given an outlet through the Athletique Club de Boulogne-Billancourt (ACBB) in Paris. This was the same amateur club that had helped Brian Robinson's old teammate Shay Elliott back in 1955 as he rode himself to a contract with its professional team for the following year. Its pro outfit was sidelined by the mid 1960s but the ACBB's amateur arm soon began taking on stars of the future by signing up untapped talent from English speaking countries like England, Ireland, Scotland and Australia, bringing them to the continent and acting as a kind of feeder club to the top trade teams of the day. It was an experiment that worked and gave European road racing a permanent facelift.

It was a platform but it still gave riders a tough introduction to Europe. They were dropped into top amateur races and expected to perform; thankfully for British cycling, many passed the test. Their shared experiences and common language helped the ACBB riders to settle as they struck up friendships, roomed together and travelled to races in groups. Even after their apprenticeships were up, the Foreign Legion's ties remained strong and by the mid 1980s many were scattered between cycling's elite continental teams.

Reliably, pedalling away in the Tour de France peloton, Barry Hoban was there to help the legion's first British success story Sherwen survive his debut in 1978. After being both Yorkshire and Britain's lone ranger for much of the '70s, Hoban was among the first to try to pass on his expertise to his home country's next great hopes. Sherwen would not go on to become a top class Grand Tour contender but a 'domestique' – a rider who helps his teams' leaders to succeed rather than going for glory himself. Nevertheless, his hard-working example set the tone as ACBB continued to nurture English-speaking hopes for years to come.

Suddenly Brits, Aussies and Americans were making an impression in top races including the Tour de France, prompting the English speaking media to take a more active interest. The closed world of European road racing was being forced open again and suddenly Fleet Street was taking a significant interest for the first time since Tom Simpson's tragic death on the Ventoux. The Foreign Legion's success stories coincided with a weak British pound, discontent under the Thatcher Government at home and the growth of holidays on the continent. It meant more and more Brits began trying their luck in France by turning up unannounced at races, while the talented youngsters passing through the ACBB production line were tried, tested and often dumped if they failed to stand out. The cross-Channel boom led many to go bust; returning home or settling into odd jobs on the continent.

Those who did return to British shores were coming back to a now thriving professional scene that was attracting some of the big European names for one-off events. Eddy Merckx lined up against Raymond Poulidor and '73 Tour de France winner Luis Ocaña for a road race at the Eastway Circuit in London in 1977. Merckx was outsprinted by 'Super' Sid Barras two years before the Yorkshireman took his first British national road race championship by beating none other than Barry Hoban in a sprint to the line. It rightly earned Barras plaudits despite Merckx being admittedly past his best.

The rapid boom in the sport's popularity, fuelled by the Foreign Legion's success, pricked up the ears of broadcasters keen to pounce on new pursuits. Channel 4 came to the table in 1983, pledging to air a new series of one-hour criterium races around British city centre circuits. The new Kellogg's Series attracted huge crowds of people who were largely new to the sport and opened the door further to stars from the continent to race the best the UK had to offer. The races were captured by static and motorbike-mounted cameras and beamed across the country, catapulting the likes of Barras into the limelight as punters packed into cities to watch the free entertainment on their doorsteps.

Barras was coming off the back of a poor '82 season and planning to retire, having bought a bike shop, before a phone call from Alan Rushton, who was promoting the Kellogg's format, changed everything. "He told me, 'if I was you I would get training'," Barras said. "I was 35 then. I started training and I won some. It was a good period of my career in the end and they were brilliant races. It was very rare that it wasn't absolutely flat out racing. It brought pro racing on a lot in Britain."

The races proved to be a final exciting chapter in Barras' career, and gave his two sons the chance to see their dad in the spotlight. Sid would wind up his powerful sprints as one of the Kellogg's Series stars; giving him some of the credit his talent had deserved years earlier. And there would be many more Yorkshire success stories to come. "I put it down to the Yorkshire grit, we've always produced good riders," Barras told me. "Yorkshire folk are dead down to earth; they just do their best, they are great people."

Four years of popular primetime city centre races followed, prompting Channel 4 to start broadcasting Tour de France highlights for the first time in 1986. But it was then that Kellogg's switched their sponsorship from city centre racing to an international stage race. The launch of the newly-dubbed Kellogg's Tour of Britain signalled the end of the Kellogg's Series of criteriums as we knew it and, despite the format being revived as the Provident Series in the early 1990s, domestic pro racing took a knock.

Nevertheless, the sport's '80s boom in Britain gave sponsors and fans the belief that a British Tour de France team could win, and win big. The blind ambition of a rotund businessman-turned-cycling team manager was a product of the wider optimism surrounding our hopes of breeding a Tour winner. Tony Capper was a rags-to-riches wheeler dealer from Stoke who had founded a taxi firm before launching and selling the haulage company ANC; the latter rapidly grew to make him a rich man. Sponsoring British pro rider Micky Morrison in 1984 opened Capper's eyes to the glamourous world of cycling and, hooked, within a year he decided to sponsor a team. Capper's team would become known as ANC-Halfords and his star sprinter would be Malcolm Elliott – a promising 25-year-old from Wadsley in Sheffield.

Malcolm Elliott wins the Sheffield Star Cycle League. August 12 1979. (YPN)

Elliott sprints to his fourth stage victory in the 1983 Milk Race at Liverpool. (YPN)

Elliott was a classy speedster known for his pedigree on the bike and his playboy lifestyle off it. He was never shy of saying he liked his beer and nights out during his racing days. He was a handsome, talented Yorkshire lad with few ties, who was living the high life. From the fast cars to the flawless sun tan, Elliott enjoyed the trappings of success – years later he would express regret over his attitude to training as a youth – although he delivered results on the bike regardless.

Elliott has credited the hills around Sheffield and South Yorkshire as being the perfect training ground for aspiring cyclists. In fact, his affinity with his hometown meant he would try to maintain a base there throughout his continental career. He saw the area as a hotbed for the sport, with the moors and snaking passes of the Peak District on his doorstep and the Derbyshire Dales only a short ride away.

He was first taught the ropes of cycling as a five-year-old by his father Jack, who was a keen touring cyclist. He'd learned to ride his sister's bike but soon persuaded his parents to buy him a machine of his own and, when he was given his freedom, would regularly head out as a teenager on 10-mile trips

Malcolm Elliott at the Milk Race in May 1987. (YPN)

to Bradfield and back. By 1976 he had joined the same touring club as his dad and was competing in his first races. He had discovered a passion for cycling.

He later joined the Rutland Cycling Club and rose through the ranks, placing second in the national junior championships in London. It was a sharp ascent and his talent was obvious as a raw youth, prompting predictions of a bright future and a place in the national junior squad. The lad from Sheffield was already travelling the world racing against future stars like American Tour de France great Greg LeMond.

Fittingly, he was given a helping hand by part of the team behind Britain's greatest cycling export to date, and a man who matured on the very same South Yorkshire hills that were Elliott's treasured training ground. While Elliott was working at Tony Butterworth's bike shop in Sheffield, Tom Simpson's former mechanic, Harry Hall, phoned as he was on the lookout for young talent to head out to France to have a go at racing for the UV Aube amateur setup in Troyes. Elliott pounced at the opportunity, moved abroad in 1980 and was picking up prize money before he joined up with his teammates as a member of GB's Moscow Olympic track cycling squad that summer. He was part of a team pursuit line-up that finished fifth.

Two years later he won double gold at the 1982 Commonwealth Games in

Brisbane, Australia, claiming the road race in a bunch sprint and a win in the team time trial. Still racing as an amateur, the road race gold strengthened his reputation before the beginning of an extremely healthy relationship with the Milk Race saw him win a record six stages in 1983.

The Milk Race was Britain's own quirky, smaller scale Tour de France and from the late 1950s to 1993 it was the biggest and best race in the country.

Elliott pictured at the Eric Gilbert Cycle races. August 23 1987. (YPN)

It was a constant, known for testing riders on the most challenging terrain Britain had to offer while giving victors the unusual prize of a bottle of frothy milk due to its sponsorship by the Milk Marketing Board. It gave a traditionally amateur British cycling scene a focal point and the country's young cyclists something tangible to aim for.

Elliott, buoyed by his victory, signed his first pro deal in 1984 but it was his time at the helm of Capper's ambitious yet ill-fated dream team that gave him exposure on the world stage as a man capable of winning Tour de France sprints. As one of the top domestic pros, he signed a deal with Capper in the back of the bulky businessman's Jaguar in 1986 that seemed almost too good to be true; and ultimately it was just that.

Capper was clear that he wanted a Tour de France adventure in what would be a short-lived foray into pro cycling, so he sent his band of international riders across Europe to compete in Classics such as the Amstel Gold and Ghent-Wevelgem, which Barry Hoban had won more than a decade earlier. He also targeted stage races like the Tour of Algarve in a bid to build a reputation that would earn them a slot in the greatest race of them all. ANC also enhanced its reputation as the top British team through sending Elliott and his teammates to big domestic races like the '86 Milk Race, which was opened up to pros for the first time and visited Harrogate and Sheffield, and the televised Kellogg's Series of city centre races.

The following year would culminate in Capper's glamorous goal, the Tour de France, largely thanks to Elliott's impressive run of results. He came third in the Dutch one-day Amstel Gold race a couple of months earlier and claimed his first overall Milk Race win in 1987. The Milk Race had been the event that had inspired Elliott from a young age. Seeing Britain's best charge along home roads was a sight to behold, and his cycling ambition was realised when he was awarded the winner's yellow jersey. The race also witnessed the emergence of another Yorkshire talent; the white jersey for best young rider went to the little known Dave Rayner, a bright prospect from Shipley who had even brighter blonde hair.

ANC's Tour de France debut came at a time when the race was bloating under the 'gigantisme' plan to expand it as a spectacle. In 1987 the race featured 23 teams rather than 14, with more than 200 riders as opposed to the 140 two years earlier, despite it being raced on the same roads, visiting the same cramped hotels and competing for the same prize money. The sudden expansion meant teams like ANC could rapidly grow and take part before imploding spectacularly, leaving unpaid cyclists in their wake.

The team was British-based and backed but had an international feel, with riders alongside Elliott including Brits Adrian Timmis and Foreign Legionnaire Graham Jones, Aussie Shane Sutton, Kiwi Steven Swart, Czech native Kvetoslav Palov and two French cyclists in Guy Gallopin and Bernard Chesnau. They were managed by ex-British racer Phil Griffiths and a prickly Belgian called Ward 'Muddy' Woutters. It was an unusual cocktail of characters that was so quickly put together that the team proved disorganised and doomed to fail from the start. The rush for last minute team ranking points to earn them a place in the Tour in the first place left many of the riders fatigued before they had even reached the start line. Meanwhile, the very prospect of tackling a mountainous three-week marathon against the world's best – most of the team having only the lower standard two-week Milk Race to compare it to – was far from attractive. On top of all that, Elliott and his ANC teammates were to take part in one of the toughest post-war Tours in history, featuring 25 days of racing and multiple draining mountain stages.

As the race got underway, it soon emerged that Sheffield sprinter Elliott was the only ANC rider who looked in a shape able to compete against the best, but that's not to say he enjoyed it. He drudged through the mountains and laboured over the line in Paris in 94th place. But he did show his class in the bunch sprints; finishing third, sixth and ninth in stage finishes at Bordeaux, Avignon and Troyes respectively. He would be the only ANC racer to return for the next year's Tour.

In his own words, that Tour – without a clear favourite after the retirement of five-time winner Bernard Hinault's a year earlier – was raced at a "crazy pace" as riders tried to stamp their authority. And having had no clear training plan under the unofficial ANC mantra of 'make it up as you go along', he felt woefully unprepared for a manic Tour which left him "suffering like a dog" to finish. "They (the other riders) were going so fast for so long and I remember one day just hanging on in a cross wind," he later told the *Yorkshire Post*. "I had a miserable first week before I started to find my feet… I was never comfortable, but I never lost the confidence that I would make it to Paris."

Despite Elliott's unexpected success, the team's overall race proved a disaster. The romanticism of Capper's ANC mission had masked a dark secret. The larger-than-life backer simply didn't have the cash to support his vision; riders went unpaid and during the Tour bailiffs raided the team's English base before he mysteriously vanished from sight ahead of the race's conclusion. ANC's ramshackle Tour was captured by a Daily Star journalist who was writing about the race from the inside. Jeff Connor's 'Wide Eyed and Legless' book depicted the team's disintegration in first-person detail, so much so that he was even drafted in to drive the team van carrying thousands of pounds of bikes and team equipment during the race.

And though the ANC story went down in Tour folklore among British fans, Elliott's adventure continued with a move to the Fagor team in 1988. He was enlisted by team leader Stephen Roche, who stunned the cycling world by winning the triple crown of the world road race championship, Giro and Tour de France in 1987. But fractions within Fagor and the loss of Roche to injury led Elliott to describe his period there as a fiasco.

The Spanish Tour, the Vuelta a España, was Elliott's first real opportunity to show his worth in a continental race wearing the Fagor colours and he took it with aplomb. During stage 17 of the '88 Vuelta from Albacete to Toledo he outgunned the field to take his first major bunch sprint win on the continent. That year's Tour de France would prove another slog, this time racing under the nominal Fagor leader Robert Millar – a top Scottish climber known for his reserved nature and 'king of the mountains' Tour triumph four years earlier.

In 1989 Elliott switched to the Spanish setup Teka, which allowed him to remain based in Sheffield while he commuted to training camps and races. This was where he truly made history, becoming the first Brit to win a Grand Tour jersey outright. He won two stages of the '89 Vuelta and the green points jersey for the best sprinter before flying home to Sheffield the same night. He also won the second annual Kellogg's Tour of Britain the same year.

But he eventually became disenchanted with cycling in Europe and made the move to the USA in 1993 to race for the Chevrolet-LA Sheriff's team – an outfit literally owned by the Sheriff of Los Angeles – in California at a time of growth for the sport across the Atlantic. In a 1993 interview with the *Yorkshire Post*, he said there were only around 10 domestic pros in the UK as sponsorship struggles made a return home unworkable. "Sponsorship is hard to get because of the recession but cycling was going backwards before the recession began to bite," he said. "There was a failure to market the sport properly when it had the chance."

He also said his time in Spain, riding the same races year-in, year-out, had gone stale and it was time for a fresh challenge. "Any rider needs more mental stimulation than that because, as with most sports, if you are not really hungry for success when you get on the bike, you might as well walk the course."

Fans at the roadside during the 1989 Milk Race. (YPN)

Nevertheless, Elliott's Grand Tour exploits put him among the greats as far as British road racing is concerned – it took until 2010 for Mark Cavendish to equal his Vuelta points triumph – but it seems winning in Europe was never really his main target. He grew up with a passion for cycling as a sport and a thirst for the pure competition of hunting down fellow sprinters at top speed, but he's never been one to profess his love for its history. The Tour de France was going through yet another mild transformation during Elliott's career and, at the time, the Vuelta and the Giro offered as much appeal if not more. Despite the prestige of the European Tours, winning on home turf appeared to drive him more than anything else.

Looking back on his continental years, it was victory in the Milk Race he'd seen fly through his home county as a child that was the realisation of a dream while his European achievements, at the time at least, were seemingly a means to an end in terms of boosting his reputation and securing his next contract. But the magnitude of those big races and the regard with which his performances are now held maybe didn't initially dawn on him, particularly given the Tour's huge reputation today.

"It's one of my regrets that when I look back on my career I didn't ride it

The start of a stage of the 1987 Milk Race at Barker's Pool in Sheffield. May 22 1987. (YPN)

(the Tour de France) more than twice," he confessed to the *Yorkshire Post* in 2014. "My career was mainly in Spain and the Vuelta a España was just as big a Grand Tour back then and the Spanish teams built their season around that. I could have ridden more Tours if I'd have chosen a different career path but I opted for the Spanish teams. With the globalisation of cycling, the Tour de France has become the biggest race. It's self-fuelling. The international sponsors all want a piece of the Tour, which has made it the race to be involved in. So my regret has probably become greater over the passage of time, because I certainly didn't feel it at the time."

Regardless, Malcolm Elliott's achievements were immense. He broke the nation's Grand Tour jersey duck, dominated bunch sprints in Britain and built on the talent he was evidently blessed with. Through the opportunism of wheeler dealer Capper, the door to international cycling creaked open but Elliott's class ensured that it became a passageway to a career winning top races at home and abroad. Little did he know that his example was driving on the young riders of his home county to push the boundaries themselves.

WEDDED TO A DREAM

Seeing homegrown cycling stars whizz through Yorkshire on the roads he knew so well both intrigued and excited a young Sheffield native called Chris Walker.

The Milk Race was an unusual sight; the huge convoy of race vehicles, the rainbow of team colours and the swarming crowds of spectators. It opened Walker's eyes to the glamour and buzz of bike racing, and presented itself as a means by which young, local riders could establish themselves on the big stage. It was mesmerising. "I had no clue what it was," he told me. "And then I saw all the cars and the riders racing past on the climbs and that was it, I thought, 'wow what is this? It's mega'."

Growing up in an area with such a strong cycling history made it easy to get drawn into giving competitive cycling a go, but Walker, unlike most of his neighbours, was not from a family with the sport weaved into its fabric. His dad was a distance runner in his spare time and Chris quite literally followed in his footsteps, displaying a natural sporting prowess from an early age. It was only when his dad suffered a knee injury and took up two wheels as a low impact alternative that Chris followed suit aged 13. The teenager was instantly hooked. He joined the Beighton Wheelers club, which counted former Olympian Brian Jolly as a member in the south east of Sheffield, and went about exploring the hills he'd grown up next door to.

"We live right on the edge of Nottinghamshire but personally when I was younger I never used to head out that way – that's where all the soft people used to go," he told me. "As soon as I started cycling I just enjoyed it, I would head out to the hills on my own. And the fact that you were up and down the climbs meant you were getting your heart rate up all the time without even knowing it. In South Yorkshire it's a lot easier to do six hours and you get a lot more out of it. Growing up here brings you on."

His passion for cycling erupted after taking part in his first fast-paced, closed circuit criterium and as a youth he won the national junior road race series two years in a row. Determined to take his talent to the next level, he left for Italian amateur racing at 19. "The guys I looked up to were the next level up from me," he said. "It was all the Sheffield riders like Malcolm Elliott, John Wainwright and Nigel Gilbert winning the national series. You see those guys and train with them and think, 'why can't I do the same?'"

Walker finished second in his first Italian race behind Franco Ballerini, who later won Paris-Roubaix twice in his career, but the reality of cycling on the continent in the mid 1980s soon became apparent. During his year in Italy he was confronted with a doping culture that shook him to the core. He turned down a pro contract and went home. "Because of what I had seen, I thought 'I'm never going to be at that level'. There were those types abroad, they got results but it wasn't sustainable," he said. "I wasn't prepared to do what they did – I know it sounds like sour grapes. Anyone that's been in that situation now says how bad it was."

Walker was emerging during what were changing times for European and British cycling. On the continent the early 1990s signalled the start of what became widely known as the 'EPO years', when widespread drug use began to distort race results and taint European cycling more so than ever before. EPO, the natural hormone erythropoietin, was a drug used to increase the production of red blood cells which carry oxygen. Its use was for a long time undetectable and allowed for quicker recovery and enhanced performance. EPO would prove the main enemy to those trying to carve out a cycling career 'clean' for much of the next two decades.

Meanwhile the ageing Foreign Legion's reign on the continent was coming to an end, with only steely Brit Sean Yates left standing by the middle of the decade as the next cohort of ambitious youngsters rolled up. Despite the dwindling British interest in Europe, Yorkshire made a brave, if slightly ill-timed, move to establish itself as a top cycling destination. Civic bosses in Leeds forked out to host the Wincanton Classic, which was the British round of a World Cup series of one-day road races that took place all over the globe. The race, which had been hosted in Newcastle and Brighton respectively in 1990 and 1991, attracted some of the best known continental cyclists and was among the most prestigious on the British calendar.

It came to the region from 1992 to 1996 and was broadcast all over Europe via satellite TV but the appetite and understanding was largely missing. The Yorkshire Evening Post carried repeated stories of discontent among regional politicians about the amount of investment required to host the Leeds Classic and it eventually surrendered the spectacle to Rochester in Kent. Leeds City Council spent £200,000 a year to host the first three editions and had to find an extra £175,000 to back the race's promoters in 1996, before having to cover a £120,000 shortfall in funding due to a lack of take-up of sponsorship. Speaking after the announcement that the race would not return for 1997, a local cycling club secretary told the newspaper: "It's a shame Leeds has lost out. The race never really got the coverage it deserved up here."

Despite the lack of uptake from sponsors, the region's cycling community

Chris Walker pictured on his way to winning the Otley Town Centre Road Race. (YPN)

FAVOURITE TRAINING RIDES

"I would head out from Rotherham towards Doncaster, Barnsley, the Strines (a series of climbs near Sheffield) and back through Derbyshire. It's worth doing and the Tour of Britain went over it. You can't believe it's just on the edge of Sheffield. It's so amazing and so tough. The run into Sheffield they did in the Tour is sharp; up and down. That was my favourite."

Chris Walker

Former Tour de France winner Stephen Roche (left) pictured with Dave Rayner ahead of the 1993 Leeds International Classic. December 8 1992. (YPN)

came out in force to watch their Grand Tour idols race local roads. Around 300,000 people lined the route of the 1996 race and the riders were keen on it too – Tour de France winner Stephen Roche posed for promotional pictures for what was billed "one of the toughest races on the calendar" in 1993. That edition covered Holme Moss and Woodhead Pass as well as visiting Harewood, the Wharfe Valley and Calderdale before finishing in Leeds city centre. The likes of Lance Armstrong, Johan Museeuw and Ballerini took part over the years and, though it was a major coup for Yorkshire, it perhaps came too soon; a theory backed up by the fact the race was removed from the British calendar altogether in 1998 and given to Germany.

Amid the Leeds Classic debate, the broader scene for British-based pro riders was suffering. The sport lost its best form of self promotion when Kellogg's ended its sponsorship of televised city centre races in 1987 and switched to backing the Kellogg's Tour of Britain international pro stage race. The initial excitement quickly fizzled out and resulted in the event being shelved in 1994 before a brief and unsuccessful revival as the PruTour in 1998 and 1999. The move to a race mirroring the quirks and complexities of continental-style racing, with its jerseys, intermediate sprints and general classification, didn't resonate with fans new to the sport who were intrigued by the high octane city centre races of the 1980s. The winding up of the Milk Marketing Board due to changes in European law in 1993 also saw off the Milk Race, compounding the problem at home.

Chris Walker could see that the British scene was unpredictable at best during his early years and sought out the continent for the glory and prestige of its races; only to find many were infected with a drug problem he never expected to face. His perception of Europe, his pre-defined career goals and his attitude to the sport completely shifted. "It was only a few close friends that kept me racing," he told me. "My bubble had burst. I had a sharp learning curve and rise from the few years I had been racing. I got seventh in the junior Worlds as a newcomer and I thought 'I want to win stages of the Tour' or at least ride it. I did think I could ride it, but for those reasons I ended up coming home. It was too big of a step down so I thought, 'done, failed', and was going to stop."

Support and a deep love for the sport eventually tempted him back into racing however, and he set about proving himself in Britain as an amateur. He eventually signed for the Water Tech-Dawes pro outfit three years later and raced alongside two riders he idolised – Sid Barras and Keith Lambert – and experienced immediate success by winning the sprint and best new pro jerseys in the first ever Kellogg's Tour of Britain.

Two years of racing at Paul Sherwen's Raleigh Banana team alongside rising star Dave Rayner offered further tests as well as some bruising beatings at major European races like Ghent-Wevelgem in 1988. Under-prepared for the challenge, the experience dented his confidence again and reinforced his thoughts on whether chasing the continental dream was something he was truly capable of.

Undeniably, Walker's career highlights came in 1991 at the Banana Falcon team under the retired Keith Lambert as team manager, where he dominated the Milk Race. He won the race overall as well as five stages, showcasing his ability and bolstering his threadbare confidence in a race he'd always dreamed of winning. The triumph inspired him to face his fears once more and return to the continent a more mature, developed rider. He famously finished second to a young Lance Armstrong after claiming four stages in the Settimana Bergamasca Italian stage race but it soon became clear the stumbling blocks were still there.

"We (Chris and Dave Rayner) both gave it another go on the continent," he said. "But the EPO thing meant they were going up the big hills on the big ring (highest gear) and we were struggling on the smallest. It didn't work out for us and we went to the US."

He and his pal Rayner's American adventure saw them race on the same IME-Healthshare team in 1993. The duo were inseparable both on and off the bike. Chris told me: "There weren't the same issues. We just enjoyed the life we had out there and enjoyed the racing."

Walker's career was one he admits was riddled with self-doubt and frustration at the apparent state of play abroad but his underlying ability on the bike was there for all to see. He came second to Tour legend Robert Millar in the 1995 British road race championships after having one too many drinks the night previous celebrating a criterium win, and he even raced alongside a young Bradley Wiggins at the amateur Team Brite three years later as his career wound down.

The question of what might have been if he had risen through the ranks at a different time could have haunted him, but his positivity and passion for the sport far outweigh any feelings of resentment he might once have harboured. He was a sign of things to come – a cyclist who adopted the sport after discovering his pedalling ability largely by chance – and his class both on and off the bike would go on to inspire his understudies and inscribe his name among a long list of pro riders to emerge from God's Own Country. "For whatever reason there's always been the riders capable of big things in Yorkshire but whatever period you are born in decides how far

you could take it," he told me. "Now it's probably the best period and there's going to be a lot more coming through."

Dave Rayner, the Shipley boy who gave Malcolm Elliott a run for his money as a junior in the '87 Milk Race, was another of the region's rising stars. His tall, gangly frame translated into smooth, powerful pedal strokes as a youngster during the riding recession of the mid 1980s. Two years Chris Walker's junior, he aspired to the same Grand Tour goals and eventually raced alongside his fellow Yorkshireman as their fluctuating careers crisscrossed. They were two young men from different backgrounds who shared a love for their sport.

Unlike his great friend, Dave had cycling in his blood. He had always had concrete ambitions of becoming a pro bike rider. Even as a scrawny nine-year-old, platinum blonde Dave pledged that he would one day follow in the footsteps of his heroes – men who were friends of his father. Dave was raised in Shipley by his mum Barbara and dad John, who in his day was a competitive cyclist himself. John is a stalwart of the cycling community in West Yorkshire, having spent decades managing Shipley frame builder Ellis Briggs' bike shop – the same firm that gave a young Brian Robinson his first sponsorship deal in the 1950s.

Dave Rayner. (YPN)

At 12 years of age Dave set in motion his sporting journey by joining the East Bradford Cycling Club before moving on to the Bradford Wheelers four years later. His ingrained passion for the sport was backed up by talent that was evident from the get-go. As he matured, he became a rider who could effortlessly rocket up hills and descend down winding roads even faster, opening the door to that fabled next step: the gamble of moving to the continent. He did so at the incredibly young age of 16 by joining the amateur setup GS Porcari-Fanini-Berti where he would improve as a cyclist by riding alongside the likes of Mario 'Cipo' Cipollini. The charismatic Italian went on to make a career out of headline-grabbing stunts and fearsome sprint finishes, which earned him 12 career Tour de France stage wins. The young Cipo, who famously wore a toga to sign into the 1999 Tour in celebration of Julius Caesar's birthday, met his match in lanky, lovable Dave Rayner. Cipo would mop up in the sprints while the blonde Brit would string out the field during races dotted with rugged climbs.

The pair successfully teamed up as amateurs and, a few months after making the brave move to Italy, the Yorkshire lad crossed the line first in Stoke to become British national junior road race champion in 1984. His Italian apprenticeship culminated in a successful 1986 season that saw him collect more than 20 amateur race wins and drive on towards his target of turning pro. Against the advice of his Italian team manager, who thought Rayner would benefit from another amateur year, the ambitious 19-year-old signed a pro deal back home with Interent-Yugo while Cipo stayed put.

Initially the decision was vindicated. Rayner collected the first of three best young rider jerseys in the '87 Milk Race won by the dominant Malcolm Elliott. An ageing Sid Barras, in his final year as a professional, rode against the rapidly developing Rayner in his impressive Milk Race debut, having seen him blossom as a Yorkshire youngster. "Dave was a skinny young lad, I remember him first coming out at 15 and he would ride until he dropped. You could see he had talent," Barras said. "He was a talented rider and a great kid."

His performances earned him a deal at leading British team Raleigh-Banana for the following season alongside teammate Walker for the first time and they instantly hit it off. "He was just one of the easiest guys in the world to get on with," Chris told me. "Everybody you talk to tells you the same. He was special."

Dave was a talented all-rounder on the bike and made waves as a friend to everyone off it. His selfless attitude and playful nature earned him a reputation as being the life and soul of the party quite quickly. Group training rides with current and former pros of the time with the Keighley Chain Gang would never be the same again.

As the 1990s beckoned, Yorkshire was still delivering the goods in terms of bike racing and Dave Rayner looked set to become the next big name to add to the list, but things were about to change. Elliott was fresh from his Vuelta triumph, young riders like Rayner and Walker were beginning to make their mark, and Ossett-born Colin Sturgess was another success story. Sturgess won the individual pursuit on the track in the World Championships as a 20-year-old in 1989 and claimed the British road race crown a year later, although his Yorkshire ties are debatable given that he moved to South Africa aged six. Sturgess' career stalled on the continent and his eventually became a familiar story of 'what ifs'.

But despite Rayner experiencing further success in the Milk Race, where he won a second consecutive best young rider jersey in 1988, he was seen more as a domestique who could work to support others at Raleigh Banana rather than a race contender in his own right. Nevertheless, he went on to win a record third consecutive Milk Race young rider's jersey in '89, finishing eighth overall, and eventually earned the move his potential had warranted after seven years of full-time racing.

The elite Dutch-based Buckler team managed by former road race World Champion and serial Classics winner Jan Raas came calling with a ticket to the biggest bike races on the planet in 1991. But the fairytale was short-lived. Again seen as a domestique, Rayner struggled in a team that mainly targeted one-day Classics rather than the stage races his skills were better suited to, and though he made his Grand Tour debut, finishing 57th in the 1991 Vuelta, Raas let him go at the end of the following season.

The decision led Rayner to move to America in 1993, which was growing off the back of the cycling success of its native three-time Tour de France winner Greg LeMond. Malcolm Elliott had also made the move to the USA, while Walker's decision to move sealed the deal for Rayner. The duo lived together but after their team ran out of cash they came home. The 1994 season, tragically, would be Rayner's last.

The endemic drug problem in the sport that Walker had witnessed did not put Dave off the scent of achieving his goals but it did get in his way. He earned his opportunities the hard way, through sheer tenacity and persistence, before they were snatched away from him at a desperately young age. Tom Barras, son of Sid, was a teenager from Laycock, near Keighley, aiming to follow in the footsteps of his father in the mid 1990s and, to him, the example that the similarly-built Rayner set made his aspirations of success on the bike seem possible. "I was 16 and Dave was in his mid 20s at the top of his game when I went out on Keighley Chain Gang rides. He would ride to meet us from Idle where he lived," Barras told me. "I wanted to be like Dave. He was very generous, he was really skinny and lanky, and so was I. He gave me his Raleigh Banana and Buckler kits and I've still got them."

Rayner's career and the humility he had shown to his understudy stayed with Barras, who followed his new-found hero's results week-in, week-out. After racing the '94 season back in the UK, Rayner married his partner and was planning for the future, with suggestions he might return to the US once more. But within just five weeks he would be dead. Rayner was assaulted outside the Maestro nightclub in Bradford in November 1994 and was rushed to hospital, but the damage had been done.

Teenage Barras was shocked by the loss of a fine Yorkshire cyclist and friend to all. "I was doing my GCSEs and it really affected me," he remembered. "I had to re-sit some as I was in Bradford Royal Infirmary with Dave when he was on life support. It was horrendous. His nickname was 'bullet proof Dave' and he was everybody's friend and so vibrant, larger than life. He didn't have to have a minute for everyone but he did. He did a lot for me. For a young bike rider, it was like being mates with David Beckham."

The cycling community was in mourning but those closest to Dave were determined to make sure he would not be remembered solely for the tragic manner in which he died. After the funeral, in a conversation between friends, family and cyclists across generations, the Dave Rayner Fund was born. In the spirit of the adventurous and driven rider, it would give British cyclists grants to help them in the struggle to succeed in road racing in continental Europe just as he had done as a brave teenager back in 1984. The county's trailblazer abroad, Brian Robinson, would chair the fund committee, while Yorkshire cycling stalwarts

Tom and Sid Barras out training together. (Bruce Rollinson, YPN)

Jonny Clay. (YPN)

including Sid Barras, Keith Lambert, Chris Walker, Wakefield's Bernie Burns and Leeds' Jonny Clay would play their part in the fund which is still going from strength to strength more than two decades on. It has so far dished out more than £1 million to help young riders achieve their dreams.

FAVOURITE TRAINING RIDES

"I love Buttertubs, stopping in Hawes and going over Kidstones. I just love riding up that valley. I particularly like going up this side of Fleet Moss and descending into Hawes. If I'm ever dead in heaven; that would be it."

Sid Barras

Before the Dave Rayner Fund came along, young British cyclists were on their own. The British Cycling Federation (BCF), as it was then known, was an amateur setup with little funding aside from members' fees to support the potential stars of the future. Amateurs competing in the Olympics, which only opened up to professionals in 1996, would have their transport and accommodation paid for and little else. Having ambitions to become a top road racer meant giving continental racing and living a punt, just as Brian Robinson had done during the 1950s. You had to have money, superhuman talent and an iron will to even have a chance of making it. There was simply little help out there.

The struggle many aspiring riders came up against was encapsulated by the stories of two Yorkshire women. By the 1990s, the women's side of the sport in particular had barely moved on from the days of Beryl Burton's dominance. Riders were amateurs, prize money was sparse and, aside from the launch of a women's version of the Tour de France, which struggled for sponsorship and repeatedly folded between 1984 and 2009, making ends meet was tough.

Lisa Brambani, from Hartshead in West Yorkshire, battled her way into elite women's cycling through her sheer ability as a pacey climber. She won a stunning four consecutive British national road race titles between 1986 and 1989, and a Commonwealth Games road race silver medal in 1990. But her results don't tell the full story. To fund her passion, she relied on sponsorship from her father, who managed a Bradford butchers, and she worked part-time as a shop assistant. It was a tough existence that forced her to travel to America to earn enough money to ride full-time until, frustrated at the lack of BCF help available, she retired aged just 23. A talent left largely unfulfilled by the sporting climate.

As a despondent Brambani shelved her short-lived career, Yvonne McGregor was launching her own. She grew up in Bradford as a bit of a tomboy, playing football with her brother before getting into distance running as a teenager and competing at county level. But it was only while she was working as a care worker for disabled people that she gave cycling a go through triathlon in her late 20s. By 1990, at the age of 29, she had come third in the National Triathlon Championships despite being a relatively poor swimmer.

An injury to her Achilles tendon put a stop to her running days and, on the advice of a local coach, Yvonne tried her hand at time trialling on the bike. Without a driving licence, she used to catch the train out to races and camp overnight, locking her bike to nearby trees so it wasn't stolen, before competing. She was skint, racing on a second-hand £80 bike and unsupported by the BCF when she rose through the ranks to chase glory in the 1994 Commonwealth Games aged 33. She managed fifth in the pursuit and surprised everyone by claiming gold in the points race. During the mid '90s she also broke two long-standing time trial records – the 10-mile and 25-mile – set by the great Beryl Burton. She was pushing the boundaries yet further.

Her inspirational exploits went further when she broke the coveted World Hour Record on a track in Colombia in 1995, while living off the compensation pay-outs from two road accidents. The advent of lottery funding finally gave her some of the support she needed ahead of the millennium and her cycling career reached its zenith in 2000. She claimed Olympic bronze in the women's individual pursuit in Sydney, before being crowned World Champion in the same event a month later. She was 39 years old.

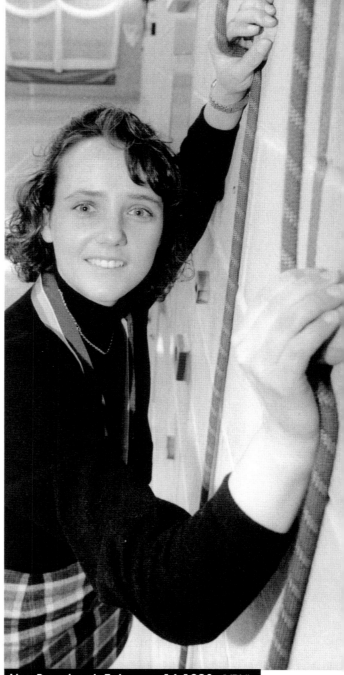

Lisa Brambani. February 16 1993. (YPN)

Brambani and McGregor showed how natural cycling talent and pure determination had to overcome a lack of support from the nation's cycling authorities. During McGregor's career, she befriended and took advice from the coaching team behind another fast-emerging talent, who was to set Britain on a course towards building the infrastructure her

Yvonne McGregor during the women's individual pursuit at the Olympic Games in Sydney. September 18 2000 (PA/John Giles) and below in 2003 (YPN)

generation craved.

Under the guidance of a progressive cyclist-turned-physiologist, part-time Wirral carpenter Chris Boardman showed what raw cycling ability and the right support could lead to during the mid '90s. Boardman was a time trial specialist who secured a ground-breaking individual pursuit gold medal in the Barcelona Olympics of 1992 that was built on a cutting edge scientific approach to training and aerodynamics that would change the sport forever. Peter Keen was the sports scientist who coached Boardman and would later set up the visionary British Cycling 'medal factory', which was perfected by his successor Dave Brailsford. Lottery-funded cycling dominance seemed a million miles away from the struggles of homegrown athletes during the '90s but winning Great Britain's first Olympic cycling gold since 1920 was the catalyst for change.

Boardman's gold, hour records and victories in the Tour de France prologue – newly-introduced short time trial stages at the start of the Tour – in '94, '97 and '98 offered hope to riders at home at a time of frustration and decline. His 1994 triumph was particularly iconic as it came in the year that Tour de France organisers gave Britain the chance to host stages of the world's greatest race for the first time in two decades; this time to commemorate the 50th anniversary of the D-Day landings.

On his Tour debut, Boardman rewrote the script for newcomers from this side of the Channel with a stunning performance. He won the 4.4-mile prologue of the Tour that started in Lille, thrashing the then three-time Tour winner and time trial specialist Miguel Indurain by 15 seconds. The surprise result came just days before the race was due to return to his homeland for stages four and five. While he couldn't hold on to the famed yellow jersey long enough to don it in Britain, he had still become the first Brit since Tom Simpson in 1962 to wear Tour de France yellow.

The 1994 edition of the great race largely proved successful for the sport in England and erased memories of the Tour's previous visit – the Plymouth bypass bore of the 1970s. But the grandeur and history of the Tour was welcomed in a slightly odd fashion. The start of the scenic 127-mile stage four from Dover to Brighton was marked by a military brass band, a troupe of American-style cheerleaders and a man parachuting from a plane to deliver a fresh yellow jersey to race leader Johan Museeuw, who was already wearing one. The race itself was nevertheless well received and, including the 116-mile stage five to Portsmouth, around two million people came out to cheer the racers on. Britain had redeemed its reputation among Tour bosses, although the public positivity surrounding the event dissipated as quickly as the riders ventured back to Northern France. The '94 race was seen as a well-received one-off; a brief holiday for the national race of the French.

Boardman's unexpected stint in yellow chimed well with British fans of cycling, who were by now a relative minority. His exploits showed that Brits could succeed in taking on Europe's best on any given day. But without a supportive avenue to attack professional cycling, the likes of Tom Barras knew they would have to do it alone. Cycling was very much in his blood and there was only ever one career he had in mind after having spent his formative years peering through the barriers of city centre criteriums trying to spot his dad, getting to know Sid's British-based pro pals and idolising the likes of Rayner and Walker before him.

He had won his first race at Rudding Park in Harrogate by the age of eight and was soon being ferried around the country, going from race to race, as a junior with the hefty tag "that's Sid Barras' son" hanging over him from the start. He persevered, won races and was eyeing up an apprenticeship as a bike racer.

But in the late 1990s it wasn't that simple. The pro scene at home was "top heavy" and lacked both opportunity and prize money. Youngsters trying to break through would probably have to do so solo.

Over the water, meanwhile, top level cycling was in a state of disarray as the depth of the doping problem that had been bubbling under the surface on the continent was unearthed. In 1998 the infamous 'Festina Affair' saw a haul of EPO and other performance enhancing drugs found in a car belonging to the Festina cycling team on the eve of that year's Tour. A series of arrests followed, the team was disqualified from the Tour and all nine of its riders confessed to drug use, casting such a shadow over the sport and the world's most famous bike race that it was initially unclear whether it would actually survive the scandal. The incident raised huge questions over the culture of doping in cycling; and it would not be the last time the sport would be rocked by riders and teams willing to cheat their way to victory.

Festina was a hammer blow to the sport's reputation, forcing many in Britain to discount cycling as an industry teeming with corruption. But for those young riders who had grown up with the sport, their passion for it never wavered. Tom Barras was determined to test his wits abroad. It was his mum and racer dad Sid who urged him to avoid banking everything on the bike during a lean spell for the sport in Britain. Tom heeded the advice, went to Loughborough University and got a degree before joining the Linda

McCartney Racing Team's under-23 squad as a trainee and being offered professional terms for the 2001 season.

Unfortunately, the British-based team bore a striking resemblance to the hapless ANC-Halfords project that capitulated in the 1987 Tour but with a modern twist. The team would be British, the riders would be vegetarian and the team would have a zero tolerance policy to drug taking. It was to be the first full-time pro team for British starlets Bradley Wiggins and Russ Downing, from Thurcroft, Rotherham, until it emerged that a series of sponsorship deals were non-existent and the whole thing fell through before the bold new venture's rider line-up was even presented to the media.

Barras, and many other aspiring pros, were back to square one. But, in the spirit of the pioneers who went before him, he felt as if chancing it across the Channel had to be done. In his mind it was a risk worth taking but he needed help, which was where the fund set up in the name of his boyhood hero Dave Rayner came in. In the seven years since Rayner's untimely death, the Dave Rayner Fund had given grants to dozens of young riders imbued with the same determination to test themselves in Europe as the Shipley racer had. Among the first riders to meet the criteria set out by Rayner's old friends and teammates was David Millar, a classy Malta-born Scot who would go on to win stages in all three Grand Tours while bringing to light the endemic drug problems still harboured within the sport. The likes of Millar and Finnish-born, York-educated climber Charly Wegelius, who were among the few Brits to appear in Grand Tours in the early noughties, were the first to benefit from Rayner's legacy and show the sport's leadership what happened when you gave talented youngsters the support they needed.

Barras would never go on to become a world-beating pro but, backed by the fund from 2001 to 2004, was given the kind of help that previous generations had gone without. He spent six years living in Belgium, learning to communicate with natives and honing skills on the bike that would earn him professional contracts for his final four years abroad. "Certainly at the time there was a gap in the market for that (the fund) and still to this day it's helping high profile riders," he told me. "It meant an awful lot that I could benefit from it. I think if it wasn't for the Dave Rayner Fund, a generation would have missed out; and British Cycling have caught on to that by taking their academy abroad. There was a generation of riders slightly older than me like Millar and then Roger Hammond and Jeremy Hunt, and they did it the hard way. They worked their way through the ranks and started winning. Brits have always done it and you could go all the way back to show that. But if you want to be a pro you've got to go abroad."

Barras lived in a loft for the entirety of his stay in Belgium, desperately scraping by to make ends meet. Money was tight but the allowance given to him by the fund helped him buy the odd luxury of a CD or a pair of trainers that made life all that more bearable. His European adventure saw him take part in amateur circuit races called 'kermesses' and learn to grind out results the hard way. More than a decade on, the memories of the challenges he faced as a bright-eyed 62kg debutant are coloured by the culture that surrounded them.

"Looking back on it I was pretty naïve because I just remember getting over there, doing my first kermesse and thinking 'how are these people riding at 55kmph?'" he told me. "You would be in the biggest gear until you cracked. The speed just goes up and up and up and to do that you realise after a few years that things might not have been on a level playing field. Dad warned me about that before I went out there. You either do it clean or you don't and I'm glad to say I chose to do it clean."

Tom Barras, Simon Gueller, Reg Haigh and Scott Thwaites pass Chelker Reservoir near Addingham. January 3 2014.
(Bruce Rollinson, YPN)

Two years of graft earned him a professional status that allowed him to race against some of the sport's biggest names including the German Jan Ullrich and legendary climber Marco 'Il Pirata' (The Pirate) Pantani, who won the Tour de France in '97 and '98 respectively. Both would later become embroiled in doping scandals, and Pantani would be found dead after a drugs binge in 2004. But looking back on a different time and rueing the decisions made by others is not something that appeals to Barras.

"You could lay in bed at night in Belgium and think 'how am I going to get that much better?' but that (doping) was just something I was not willing to do," he said. "You could blame the world and coaching and people for taking drugs and think 'that's why I wasn't a Tour de France winner' but you make your choice."

He left Belgium with no regrets in 2006, having matured as a rider and accomplished goals on the bike, but the realisation that he might not make it at the top level drove him to set up small web design and coaching businesses. He moved to Leeds and retired at the age of 28, before seeing first-hand the impact that lottery-funded British Cycling success had had on the professional road racing scene at home while he was away. During Barras' continental crash course, Britain had claimed Olympic track cycling golds through the likes of Jason Queally in Sydney in 2000 and Bradley Wiggins and Chris Hoy in Athens in 2004, and produced World Champions in countless men's and women's disciplines on the track; and that progress was beginning to translate to the road.

The British Cycling revolution came off the back of the work between Boardman and Keen that yielded the 1992 Olympic individual pursuit title. Keen's scientific approach to track racing, studying nutrition and aerodynamics while making use of heart monitors and SRM meters to record the amount of power riders were putting through a bike's cranks, changed the game for British cyclists. He acted as the BCF's unpaid national coach from 1989 to 1992 before becoming its first performance director as the advent of lottery funding came in with the promise it would lead to more Olympic gold medals. He also devised what became known as the 'World Class Performance Plan' to implement his coaching philosophy on a wider scale – a foundation that would be built upon by his successor Dave Brailsford – as the BCF continued to evolve. It was rebranded British Cycling in 2001.

A lot had changed and it had suddenly become feasible that a British-based pro could make a decent living by plugging away in domestic races once more. Within months of Barras' return to Yorkshire, he was training and racing, and before long wannabe sponsors were tapping him up. By 2008 he was a professional once again. He told me: "I came over to England in 2006 to leave a scene that was dwindling and found one that was growing. When I started training in 2007 and started racing, people started offering me bikes and money that hadn't been there six or seven years ago."

The pool of talent in Yorkshire was also swelling. His training rides alongside his dad, who remains an active masters rider, echoed the routes of his professional predecessors. They would meet at the iron bridge in Ilkley, which is equidistant from his Leeds home and his dad Sid's Steeton farmhouse, and ride the back roads through to Bolton Abbey and the Dales beyond in all weather. Before long they were joined by some of Barras senior's old racing pals and, as the years progressed, up-and-coming riders such as Burley-in-Wharfedale's Scott Thwaites, Leeds' Josh Edmondson and Keighley's Tom Moses have tagged along on their journeys to becoming pro road racers. The 'Iron Bridge Crew' is still alive and thriving to this day. In fact, when I spoke to Tom Barras he'd just returned from an ice cold jaunt with them.

During a career that spanned nearly two decades, Barras raced for 10 pro teams and amassed more than 100 elite wins at varying levels at home and abroad. His final year on the pro scene in 2015 was with NFTO, a Yorkshire-based outfit with a history of backing White Rose riders such as Edmondson, Sheffield's Adam Blythe and Rotherham's Downing brothers. Such a team's rise through the pro ranks on home turf would have been hard to believe in his younger years searching for a living from the sport he loved. He saw the lows and the highs of Yorkshire and Britain's modern cycling journey, and he earned the right to do so. His survival on the continent and his journey back home ran parallel with a gritty mentality and passion for bike riding; traits he sees among many of the next generation of Yorkshire pros.

"Traditionally people from round here would be in mills, on farms or they'd be down the pit or fishing, and they'd have to live off what they had and that isn't easy," Tom told me. "There is a spirit among Yorkshire people that doesn't go away. There is a drive in us to succeed, there is an element of showing no weakness and cracking on; that's why we make good bike riders."

Ed Clancy wins the 2011 Colne Grand Prix in Lancashire ahead of Dean Downing. (Ben Parsons, YPN)

FUNDING REVOLUTION AND OLYMPIC OPTIMISM

The golden achievements of Chris Boardman sparked a renewed optimism about Britain's chances of turning a history of brave underdogs into international domination in the future.

The foresight of Peter Keen and the decision to break down track cycling in particular into controllable variables like the power that a rider puts through the pedals, the aerodynamics of a cyclist's position on the bike and the points at which riders produce lactic acid were changing the sport beyond recognition. British Cycling was tearing apart the form book, the accepted norms were being challenged and riders from a land once marginalised by the continentals were starting to shine on the world stage.

By 2003, former amateur road racer Dave Brailsford, who had been acting as an advisor to British Cycling, took over as performance director from Keen and continued to turn the sport on its head. He is credited with the famed "aggregation of marginal gains" concept – the idea that if you broke down everything that goes into pro cycling and improved each aspect by one per cent, the collective improvement would be significant. This would stretch to the advent of bringing in a sports psychologist and a nutritionist as well as tweaking training and bringing in the likes of the now-retired Boardman to head up the jokingly named 'Secret Squirrel Club' to test technological advances that could aid riders, from aerodynamic kit to innovations in riding position. This was a new dawn for cycling in Britain.

The Commonwealth Games in Manchester in 2002 had given track cycling a further boost following the country's Sydney Olympic success and now it was time to harness the hype and breed a generation of riders who would be given the chances their predecessors were not. The cycling governing body had launched a talent spotting plan that saw scouts go into schools and test the aptitude of youngsters to cycling; children who might never have ridden a bike competitively before.

Its most significant step in aiding road racers was the development of an academy for the best riders aged 18 to 23 in the country. Based at Manchester's Velodrome, the academy was the brainchild of former pro and red-headed motivator Rod Ellingworth. It involved putting a small annual intake of Britain's most promising young riders through a gruelling schedule of track and road training that would cross over into the Peak District – the tough hills of South Yorkshire, Derbyshire, Staffordshire and

Cheshire that helped to mould some of the greatest British road racers in history. They would live and breathe the sport, be grouped together and put up in shared houses in Manchester, riding to the velodrome every morning and learning skills essential to aspiring cyclists. One of the most vital lessons to those with international aspirations was to learn the language of cycling: French.

It was an ambitious boarding school for raw talent that had been backed up by public funds, and its future was dependent on Olympic success. It had the overarching aim of generating Olympic cycling medals for Team GB, which were most likely to come on the track where there are more events. But learning the ways of the track is widely recognised as a way of building the foundations of stamina and form that can lead to long-term success on the road; the careers of Tom Simpson and Barry Hoban are testament to that.

The announcement of a British Cycling Academy, offering top equipment, coaching, an allowance and accommodation for two years, was a massive opportunity for the first intake of six young cyclists. One of the lucky few to make it on to the programme was a ginger-haired 18-year-old from Yorkshire. Ed Clancy's story sums up how British Cycling's proactive and well-financed approach helped to unearth a talent that might otherwise have slipped through the net.

Born in Barnsley before eventually moving to Holmfirth, Clancy cycled for the fun of it as a youth. His first bike was a black and white hand-me-down BMX that used to belong to his brother, before his first racing bike entered the fray as a means of climbing the ample hills around their home town. Before long 14-year-old Ed had joined the Holme Valley Wheelers cycling club but by his own admission he was "more interested in doing wheelies than going fast" to start with. The club's weekly Wednesday night 10-mile time trial became his focus and, though he found it tough going to begin with, his competitive nature and natural power on the pedals saw him improve quickly and dramatically. The Wheelers became a staple part of his home life, fellow club members would ferry him to and from races, and in the year 2000 a trip to the Manchester Velodrome with a club member who was also one of his Shelley High School teachers gave him his first taste of track cycling. "I was inspired by Rob Hayles (pro track and road racer) on that day, little realising that he'd become a teammate," he told the *Yorkshire Post* early in his career.

At 15 he was urged by clubmates to attend a British Cycling Talent Team try out day, where he was assessed for skills and traits transferable to cycling to get on to a scheme that supported gifted young riders. By the end of the session the governing body's coaches well and truly had him on their radar. His tall frame and inherent power were perfect for a sprinter, so when the academy arose he got an interview for one of the six places up for grabs in late 2003.

At the time he was studying engineering at Huddersfield Technical College and heading towards a career in industry. If the academy system had not been so perfectly timed to coincide with Clancy's development, the Yorkshireman's potential might well have been missed. But he was one of the six selected and scored joint highest in a matrix of test results, from motivation to raw physical power output, along with a certain Mark Cavendish – a young sprinter from the Isle of Man who had been plotting to follow the well-trodden path to the continental amateur road scene before the academy call came.

Cavendish, who would go on to win a record number of Tour de France stages and become the world's most lethal sprinter on the road, had Yorkshire ties of his own. Although born and raised as a Manxman, his mother grew up in Harrogate where he'd holidayed as a child and he was even a boyhood Leeds United fan. Clancy and Cavendish hit it off, although the former's allegiance to Huddersfield Town might have been an early stumbling block.

Clancy, Cavendish and fellow recruit Bruce Edgar were put up in Fallowfield, on the outskirts of Manchester, in one of the two rented academy houses. Cavendish has since described his old housemate as having strength seemingly from another planet and an endearingly different personality to match, in what sounded like a period filled with as much drama and high jinks as you'd expect in university halls. It provided at least some escape from their relentless training and racing programme. They were generally pretty skint, the house was full of flat-pack furniture and cleaning was simply not on the agenda.

An average academy day back in Manchester would consist of a 7am ride through city traffic to the velodrome, long stints on the roads through the Peak District from 8am, before returning for lunch, then a two-hour French lesson and three hours of track sessions until 6pm; potentially followed by evening races. The academy's baptism of fire abroad then included regular road racing trips and battles on the notoriously difficult 'Six-Day' circuit, in which riders compete in pairs over six days of intense track racing. Only the most talented and driven would survive.

Clancy learned to hold his own on the huge ascents of Holmfirth and the

South Yorkshire Peaks but always felt more at home on the track. Giving absolutely everything in individual and team sprint events was where he excelled. At around 80kg and 6ft 1ins tall, he's not built to glide up climbs like the fabled Tour mountaineers. Weeks after his 20th birthday he won gold for GB in the team pursuit at the 2005 Track World Championships in Los Angeles, and since then he hasn't looked back. He has gone on to win five World Championship golds – four team pursuits and one omnium.

He won his first team pursuit gold medal at the 2008 Beijing Olympic Games alongside Paul Manning, Bradley Wiggins and Geraint Thomas, who joined the British Cycling Academy the year after Ed and has since gone on to win the prestigious Paris-Nice stage race on the road. Clancy's team broke

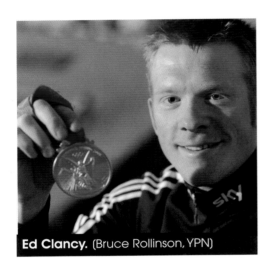

Ed Clancy. (Bruce Rollinson, YPN)

the world record for the event twice by building on his rocket-like starts. In a team pursuit the first rider to race at the front of the four-man group punches a hole in the air so his teammates can conserve energy by riding in his or her slipstream. Clancy's evident class and stamina emerged as he led the team deep into the second circuit of the race – more than the single circuit expected of a 'lead-out' man – establishing an unassailable lead over the opposition. "Every time you change the front man costs you a fraction of a second," he explained afterwards. "It's all about fractions. The closer you are to the guy in front, the better. There's no room for error. Fortunately, I haven't had a bad accident. Teamwork is key. In Beijing, I was just relieved it was over. It's what we had been working towards for so long."

Despite his success on the track and role in Team GB's rise, Clancy simply considers himself an adrenaline junky at heart, enjoying mountain biking and motorcycling off-road. He is an unassuming man with a raw power that has been harnessed by a British Cycling system that has changed the sport and popularised it once again. In all, he has won five world and three Olympic titles – that's some haul for a thrill-seeker who "started cycling for a laugh".

While it unearthed rough track diamonds like Clancy, the academy setup also helped to mould young road racers who grew up obsessed with the sport; Cavendish was one of those. The Manxman maintains that even

Ben Swift racing in the Manx International Cycle Grand Prix 2016. (YPN)

without the support of British Cycling he would have followed in the footsteps of the likes of Tom Simpson and set about getting himself noticed in amateur races in Belgium or France. And, with a career record of 30 Tour de France stage wins and victory in the monumental Milan-San Remo one-day race, it is pretty difficult to doubt him. He spent two years working in a bank to save up solely to fund his leap of faith before the call to join up with the academy came. Cavendish eventually went it alone on the road after his British Cycling education, and he was joined by a different Yorkshire academy starlet along the way.

Ben Swift, from Throapham, Rotherham, also grew up with a deep passion for riding his bike; he even entered his first race at Rother Valley Country Park aged just three-and-a-half in 1990. His father, a maintenance engineer who rode alongside him that day, was a keen cyclist himself and introduced the youngster to the world of two wheels first through mountain biking and BMX riding. Swift junior simply thrived on the thrill he got from riding at speed, and joined the ranks of local cycling fanatics early on.

"There has definitely been a cycling community as far as I can remember in Yorkshire," he explained. "It's the only place I know in Britain that's been like that all my life. It's part of the culture here."

Bike riding was a constant topic in the Swift household and his neighbourhood proved to be a micro-community of top domestic pros – men he now realises were his first cycling heroes. "When I really think about it, when I was young it was the guys in the local area that inspired me," he said. "John Tanner (two-time British national road race champion) lived down the road, Russ and Dean Downing lived in the next village along and Chris Walker lived nearby."

That local interest blossomed partly thanks to his dad's enthusiasm for the sport. They would go to local races together and nine-year-old Ben was even once a mascot for Walker and Downing's Team Invader during the mid '90s. The whole atmosphere and buzz of the races spurred his interest, while a family friend who collected domestic bikes and jerseys did even more to stoke the fire. Ben explained: "We used to stop at his house and dad would chat to him downstairs and I would go up into his loft and see all the kit he had. It felt like it was close to me even before I started watching the pros on TV."

Over the coming years he became even more immersed in the sport; racing home from school to watch the international sprinters he drew further inspiration from – the Spaniard Oscar Freire and Australian Robbie McEwen in particular – fighting it out during pulsating Tour de France stage finishes on TV. He bought into the romance of the continent and jumped straight back on his bike after the televised highlights finished and toured South Yorkshire on his own. He was besotted.

As a youngster he raced for cycling clubs in Ashfield, Mossley and Scunthorpe, often sneaking out of school early to join the club runs he came to love from the age of 12 onwards, while racing against Britain's best juniors all over the country and beyond. A golden generation of future pros became his rivals and friends. "I only have to look at old pictures to see Geraint Thomas, Ian Stannard and Peter Kennaugh camping together with us at races as kids," he told me. "It's nice to look back at that. We're all still doing the same but making money out of it. We have still got that same passion."

The aptly-named speedster rose through the ranks incredibly fast. Recognising there was a gap between the standard of road racing in

Britain and abroad, he and his pals joined forces to travel to Belgium for races on weekends to give them a taste of what they could expect long-term. They had a considered plan to become pros, even when it meant spending weekends abroad before heading back home for school on a Monday. "We realised if we wanted to keep pushing we needed to be racing abroad," he said.

Despite his progress and commitment, Ben was initially knocked back by British Cycling. He failed a trial for the British Cycling Talent Team because he struggled in tests measuring a rider's power. It was a hard pill to swallow. "When it came around I knew the sport. Everybody was saying 'you'll easily do it and get on it' but I didn't make the cut," he remembered. "I was pretty devastated; I was pretty much one of the only people out of my friends who didn't get on it. People I was beating were on it in front of me."

But he bounced back and secured a place on the governing body's Olympic Development Programme on the track. He won national junior track titles in 2004 and the year following, forcing his way into the second batch of riders to join the British Cycling Academy in 2005. Dividing their time between Manchester and Tuscany, Swift excelled on the Italian roads and developed into a strong all-rounder with a blistering sprint and a natural ability to negotiate his way into winning breakaway groups – a skill that could prove decisive in one-day races. Swift refused to take his world class cycling education for granted though, well aware of the opportunity he stumbled upon that bypassed his heroes growing up. "There was definitely a change and push in British Cycling and I'm quite fortunate to have been in that era," he told me. "I always speak to people like Russ (Downing) and I know he didn't have the same opportunities I had when he was growing up. He's had a brilliant career and made the most of everything that he can but it's amazing how different it would have been for him and others with that support structure. We are quite fortunate."

Swift was shaping up as a Classics contender of the future right before Ellingworth's eyes and nothing was going to get in his way. By the mid noughties it seemed, whether they favoured the track or the road, Yorkshire riders were getting used to a level of progression and success that was the stuff of dreams for their predecessors. Being at the centre of a comprehensive talent nurturing model that was taking potential and turning it into results made kicking on and scoring huge international victories seem like the logical next step in their development. "I knew I didn't want to do anything other than pro cycling but I never kind of said 'I will be that'," he told me. "It just kind of came as I got more into it. It almost felt a bit like destiny; that it was my path."

Russ Downing pictured on his way to winning the 2002 Otley Town Centre Road Race, June

THE LONG HARD SLOG

British Cycling's sports science boffins were plotting a cash-rich course to cycling gold medals and long-term glory on the road, but the advent of an academy came too late for a generation of riders left in its forward-thinking wake.

The whole academy system was geared towards instilling valuable lessons in precocious young talents through training and the classroom, as well as a sense of optimism and confidence that had bypassed domestic cycling hopefuls probably since the glory days of the Foreign Legion.

While the likes of Clancy, Cavendish and Swift were powering around the track and learning French at Manchester Velodrome, the likes of Dean and Russ Downing were fighting to make a name for themselves on the continent after battling with years of struggle and self-doubt. They were in their mid 20s by the time governing body bosses managed to form a blueprint for success that could be replicated nationwide. But while they may have missed out on a star-studded schooling, the Downing brothers made up for any disadvantage with a deep devotion to the sport they had wanted to commit their lives to from the outset.

The pair grew up together in Thurcroft on the outskirts of the industrial town of Rotherham. As the sons of an amateur grass and hard track bike racer who competed at carnivals during the 1980s, it was only a matter of time until the brothers gave it a go themselves. Their dad was a hard worker with a love for cycling. He worked as a carpenter performing repairs at Thurcroft Colliery until it closed in 1991. It forced him to reassess and use his redundancy money to help him open his own bike shop in the area.

Dean, who is the eldest by three years, got his first racing bike at the age of eight and Russ followed closely behind. Inspired by their dad, they cheered him on at race meets as kids, standing at the centre of the oval tracks, watching him whizz around the bends, wondering when they would get their chance. The bike shop only intensified their fascination with the sport but any bonuses of having a dad with access to top equipment would have to be earned through getting stuck in. "I used to have my own bowl in the back of the shop and I'd spent my time mending inner tubes," Russ told me. "He (dad) had me working for my kit. I bought my first mountain bike through it but I had to work all the hours God sent for it."

Before long they had followed in their dad's tyre tracks and joined clubs of their own, earning their stripes competing against the best young riders to come out of Sheffield, South Yorkshire and eventually the country. And those formative years of racing for racing's sake are still memories they hold dear. They never lost that love for the bike. But the outlook for aspiring British pros was nevertheless bleak by the time the Downing brothers had matured into men and were physically ready to turn pro in the late 1990s. Too early for the benefits of lottery support, the pair had convinced themselves that becoming top level professional road racers was nothing more than a pipedream.

Upon leaving school, Dean tried to balance the lure of bike racing with the necessity of earning building trade qualifications at college for two years. Some success on the bike, such as winning his first national grass track racing title as a 17-year-old, was tempered by failing to make GB's team for the World Junior Track Championships the year after. So he opted to prioritise his studies and do a four-year construction management degree at Sheffield Hallam University. Cycling was on the backburner and after his graduation he moved to London for a job in industry. Russ, meanwhile, was training to become a joiner in the late '90s, equally unconvinced about whether a career on two wheels would pay.

Nudges in the direction of the saddle would come from different sources for the pair. Dean was 18 months into his construction job when he was pulled aside by his manager at work in 1999 and told to make the most of his natural ability as a cyclist. Now in his mid 20s, it was his last chance. He packed his bags for Australia to train full-time, before heading for Belgium where he competed on the same amateur circuit Tom Barras was frequenting for three years. He then returned to Britain and by 2005 had signed his first pro deal domestically. Dean managed to make a career on the growing British scene before and after another brief stint abroad. During his career he won British Criterium Championship titles in 2002 and 2008, and also became British Madison Champion – a discipline in which two-man teams complete 200 laps of a track between them – alongside his brother in 2003.

Russ took advice from one of his cycling heroes when he committed to chasing his pro ambitions. Years earlier he had joined Thurcroft Cycling Club as a youth before graduating to Dinnington Racing Club near Sheffield, which had a big track racing reputation at the time and also had a small pro road team. Both Russ and his brother were sponsored as young riders before Russ' breakthrough at the under 16s national championships. He won medals in every discipline over 10 days of competition.

Those early results began to convince him that he could make a success of himself as a pro bike rider but – as was the mood among young Brits in the lull of the EPO years – Russ' upbringing on the bike was laced with self-doubt. South Yorkshire had produced some great riders who had flourished at home but struggled abroad; many because they refused to subscribe to the doping norms they stumbled upon. There were few British trailblazers making their mark in Italy, France or Belgium that made that dream seem attainable. "There was no given route to take to be a pro bike rider," Russ told me. "The feeling was you needed to be ultra-special to be a pro bike rider when I was coming through. Now it's really different."

At 17 he started a four-year apprenticeship as a joiner at a local steelworks, while living with his parents and racing at every opportunity in his spare time. He got to know fellow South Yorkshire native and former Milk Race winner Chris Walker, who was winding down at the end of his career but still active on local roads. Walker, who would become a teammate of Russ' at Team Brite in 1998, immediately spotted the potential in the agile stage racer and urged him to down tools as an apprentice. The advent of lottery funding in '98 also coincided with Russ' progress domestically and he was soon on the radar of the British governing body's bosses as one for the future; but he had always needed that injection of belief.

"Chris had taken me under his wing," he told me. "I was still working but he said 'you're going well; your results are good'. He talked me into going full-time and that helped me. I learned pretty quickly at Team Brite and it made it a lot easier. If it wasn't for Chris, I'd still be working in steelworks and thinking I wasn't good enough. I looked up to Chris – he knew what it took."

His fast development on the bike quickly turned him into hot property. He was training on the hills he'd fallen in love with at home and turning a commitment to the sport into something far more tangible. And he credits growing up around harsh country road ascents and stunning Peak District scenery, with moulding him into a man comfortable on short, punchy climbs and powerful on the road. "The hills really did influence me; it's made me the rider I am," he said.

Russ was 21 when he signed his first major contract with the same doomed Linda McCartney Cycling Team that had offered a young Tom Barras and superstar-in-the-making Bradley Wiggins a route into professional sport in 1999. He travelled abroad with the team for some early amateur races amid talk of huge investment and the promise of a bigger, brighter future for Britain's best young pros, before signing a three-year deal from the 2001 season onwards.

But the truth had been spectacularly embellished and Russ' hopes were

Russ Downing racing in the 19th Otley Town Centre Cycle Race. June 16 2004. (YPN)

dashed. He had turned up to the unveiling of the team line-up in London, having packed his bags for an exotic four-week training camp that was due to follow, when the news filtered through that there was in fact no team and no contract after all. For a young rider not blessed with huge self-confidence it was a hammer blow, and could have derailed his career entirely; it certainly threatened to until a French amateur team – linked to top coach Rod Ellingworth – offered him an escape route. "They rang my parents' house and said 'would we be interested?'. I had totally lost my head after McCartney's and I was drinking a bit too much," he told me. "I didn't know what to do. They said they'd give me an apartment in France but they wouldn't be able to pay me."

The collective spirit of the Yorkshire cycling scene came to his rescue. The increasingly important Dave Rayner Fund fittingly agreed to fund the Thurcroft athlete for the year. Dave's old cycling pals were not going to stand by as a top talent from the county was denied the opportunity to shine. Russ' natural ability and desire to make a name for himself ultimately paid off. He won more than a dozen races during his cash-strapped debut season in France but the battle to get that elusive chance in an elite team, such as the one promised to him by the Linda McCartney mirage, was only just beginning.

"I was kind of worried," he said. "There weren't that many pros, a handful of British pros, and no one was getting recognition. I became national road race champion in 2005 and thought that might break me into a bigger team, I went to live in Belgium for DFL Cycling and won big races but still struggled to get in. Every time I went over the water I felt like I was good enough but I wasn't breaking in."

It would take a decade of plugging away to finally get given a chance to get regular opportunities to test his wits against the men recognised as the world's best cyclists in the legendary stage races of the continent. In the meantime, he put the miles in for several teams abroad and at home as the domestic pro scene started to flourish off the back of cycling's growing popularity. It was improving to such an extent that it was even attracting some familiar faces who wanted to give pro bike riding another crack.

The so-called playboy of the late 1980s, Malcolm Elliott, had returned from his mid '90s exile in US road racing rejuvenated with a fresh love for cycling and a renewed desire to get out there and train. In 2003 at the age of 41, Elliott was ready for his second wind having retired six years earlier. He initially returned to compete in masters' races but soon found he could carry on doing what he did best; winning bunch sprints. He has since spoken of how he actually enjoyed riding and training more during his comeback than during his first career, in which the sport he loved had turned into somewhat of a chore. Elliott's return gave a second glimpse at his class on the bike, winning races against riders two decades his junior. Arguably his greatest win during his comeback was clinching the International CiCLE Classic race in 2007 where he beat the likes of Dean Downing and Mark Cavendish at the age of 45. He retired again in 2011.

Elliott's reinvigorated comeback was another positive at a time of progression for cycling in Britain. Cavendish, fresh from his academy apprenticeship, eventually decided to go it alone by joining the T Mobile professional team, which was among the best on the continent at the time. His debut Tour de France came in 2007 – a year that reinforced the message that cycling was here to stay in Britain. For the first time since the short-lived success that proved to be Britain's hosting of two Tour stages in 1994, the greatest race on earth was coming back to Blighty. This time, however, we would be getting our very first Grand Départ – a ceremonial launch that usually sees the three-week race start in a different country.

The foresight of the likes of Keen and Brailsford in rethinking how best Britain could succeed in track cycling was resulting in advances on the road in the early noughties. British Cycling track talents were making waves in continental pro teams and a growing portfolio of Olympic track medals helped to persuade Tour organisers that venturing over the Channel could enhance the race and the brand. Academy graduates Cavendish and Thomas would both take their places on the start line in 2007 as well as David Millar and Bradley Wiggins, who had both tasted success on the track with the British team and were by now well-established on the road.

Meanwhile, professional road racing in Europe was trying to give fans hope that its teams had cleaned up their act after the EPO years and a foray into the British Isles was a brave new step. A picturesque five-mile time trial course from Whitehall to The Mall, taking in Parliament Square, Buckingham Gate and Constitution Hill along the way, proved the perfect Tour send off before a 126-mile stage from London to Canterbury via Kent impressed again. More than two million people turned out to wave on the riders, while the fanfare of the race boosted the South-East's regional economy by an estimated £88 million. The Tour's organisers had got their wish of a fresh fan base for their race, even if the phantom of doping had not yet fully vacated the sport – three riders were caught cheating in the '07 Tour.

The sport's transition from its gory recent past to a new dawn of transparency had not proven to be a simple one. The early noughties, while fruitful for British track cyclists and the popularity of the activity in all forms at home, were littered with scandal as the sport tried to drain itself of the drug-riddled contradictions of the past. Seven-time Tour de France winner Lance Armstrong, who later admitted blood doping to an extent that annulled all of his yellow jersey triumphs, had retired in 2005 but rumours and speculation over his conduct amid repeated denials of cheating cast a prolonged shadow over the sport.

But for those who were born and raised wanting to test themselves in the world's most famous races, the romance and history associated with European Classics and Grand Tours meant the long battle to compete in them was worthwhile. Russ Downing's decade of pro exploits aimed at earning that step up the ladder eventually paid dividends. He earned his chance particularly thanks to two years of results which included winning the 2009 Tour of Ireland overall, beating a field that included Lance Armstrong and Mark Cavendish. The elite opportunity came as part of the next step in the British Cycling plan to transform the country's role and reputation on the international cycling scene; it came through Team Sky.

In January 2010 the world's media gravitated towards Millbank Tower in London for the launch of the latest British-based professional cycling project. And again, nine years on from the last false dawn, the big names included Russ Downing and Bradley Wiggins, but the déjà vu ended there. Team Sky was unveiled and the grand ambitions and concrete targets were laid out in front of the world and the riders. There were no smoke and mirrors; this was the launch of British Cycling chief Dave Brailsford's ambitious plan to ensure a clean British rider won the Tour de France with a British team within five years.

After more than a century of frustration in the world's toughest cycling test, the wider sporting world could have been excused for scoffing at what generations of Brits had failed to do since the Tour's inception; but this seemed different. It was a project backed to the tune of a reported £30 million and devised with Brailsford's ethos of turning marginal gains into big victories at its heart. As it turned out, Team Sky would bring the kind of innovation and foresight to road racing that British Cycling had brought to track cycling.

It was a mix of using advances in equipment, sport science-led rider preparation and training, and the nurturing of pure talent that would challenge the sport's entrenched traditions. There were simple things like making riders warm down on static bikes after races to aid recovery and bringing in British Cycling's nutritionist and sport psychologist to ensure the

Riders pictured on the Cow and Calf climb at Ilkley during stage four of the 2007 Tour of Britain from Rotherham to Bradford. September 13 2007.
(Bruce Rollinson, YPN)

riders were mentally and physically in peak condition. A state-of-the-art battle bus featuring flat screen TVs, showers, beds, washing machines and air conditioning was also commissioned so the athletes could live in comfort on the road. Team Sky's fine-tooth comb approach even saw experts investigate a pillow that would help riders get the best sleep possible, test for the most effective type of massage gel and teach riders how best to wash their hands to avoid infection.

For Russ Downing it was the culmination of everything he had worked for. "There was a feeling straight away of 'this is unbelievable'," he said. "They go on about marginal gains but they just had everything dialled in. There was never any issue with anything. We got phones and laptops, and if you ever needed to get a question answered you could get in touch with anybody instantly; there was no stone unturned. You just got on with your job and did your races. I just wish it would have come 10 years earlier, but I still thought 'let's make the most of the opportunity'."

He did just that and made history by becoming the first British Team Sky race winner, claiming a stage of the French two-day Criterium International. He also won the Tour de Wallonie and a stage of the Tour of Qatar at the age of 32. "They said it was too late or maybe I was a bit too old," he told me. "I didn't get massive support and was getting thrown around leading guys out (setting up other riders' final sprints) but every opportunity I got I took it."

Despite his form, he missed out on a place in that year's Grand Tours. His place in what was fast becoming one of the biggest teams in the sport would only last another 12 months but, in spite of his disappointment, he was handed a place in the 2011 Giro d'Italia. It was the Grand Tour he'd always aspired to ride after spending a year earlier in his career racing on the country's challenging hills. Sean Yates, the team's manager at the time, told Russ it looked set to be one of the toughest Giros in living memory; packed with relentless mountain climbs. Russ relished it, claiming eighth in one stage and battling through to the finish despite sustaining a few broken ribs in a mid-race crash. "It was unreal. It was always a big passion of mine," he added. "They would have had to drag me off the bike to stop me finishing."

He refused to let the disappointment of leaving the team put a dampener on what had been a successful two years. He regrouped and, at the time of writing, is still a pro bike rider with the JLT Condor team that is also home to track sprinter Ed Clancy, who trains for the track by competing in town centre criteriums. Russ' latest team comes after he spent a year as teammates with his brother Dean at the same NFTO outfit that became home to Tom Barras.

Downing's departure from Sky marked a further period of evolution at the team. They had laid the foundations of a strong team and were now going to make an assault on the most prestigious road races on the professional calendar with the next generation of riders. Bradley Wiggins was the star man, while young pretenders such as the Kenyan-born British climber Chris Froome were deployed in support roles. Another one of the men tasked with taking Team Sky forward was Ben Swift, the talented academy graduate from Rotherham who had also been a member of the outfit since its inception.

Swift had earned his place by developing into an astute member of the pro peloton after leaving the British Cycling comfort blanket. He first became a trainee at the Barloworld pro team and impressed by winning the king of the mountains polka dot jersey in the 2007 Tour of Britain as a teenager, but his progress was not enough to score a permanent contract as a professional. Still aged just 19, he returned to the British Cycling Academy for a third year and honed his skills while taking part in the road race as a member of the Team GB Olympic squad at the Beijing Games of 2008. Overall that year he claimed 28 top 10 finishes. Reinvigorated, he once again left the British safety net by joining the Russian Team Katusha in 2009.

He made his Grand Tour debut at the Giro d'Italia just five months into his continental career and claimed a stunning third place on stage two, but Swift's upbringing in the academy had demystified such fabled races. For him it was a step on a broader path. "I just got on with it," he said. "It was just a bit weird finishing third in a stage; I was taking it day by day. For me it was just part of the process."

Pro cycling had been deconstructed for a driven new generation of British riders, who felt that winning big was well within reach. The days of universal self-doubt were over. And after his impressive debut at Katusha, Team Sky came calling in 2010. Ben had flown the nest but the lure of joining forces with the friends he had shared the junior journey with, and the promise of future success proved enough to take him back to Britain. "It felt a bit strange – this idea of a big British team – and it was pretty exciting but at the same time I had gone on to something different," he told me. "I felt like I had turned professional on my own; Katusha was my first real step away from that comfort zone. We had been in this secure bubble for so long and I thrived away from it and made the most of it. In the end coming to Team Sky was quite surreal because we had been racing together since we were eight years old, and now we were professionals."

FOLLOW THE RAINBOW

The growing optimism and evident talent in the British ranks since lottery funding changed the game inspired another challenge. Rod Ellingworth, the man who had offered Russ Downing a lifeline after the Linda McCartney debacle in 2001 and was behind the British Cycling Academy, wanted the current golden generation of British road racers to rewrite history. He was focused on a bid to emulate one of Britain's greatest achievements on a bike to date: Tom Simpson's 1965 road World Championship win.

Winning the Worlds is arguably the second biggest prize in the sport behind the Tour de France's yellow jersey, offering the victor the chance to wear the coveted rainbow jersey at every road race for 12 months. Ellingworth's ambitious 'Project Rainbow Jersey' plan involved bringing together the country's best pro road racers on one GB team and making the Worlds a collective focus. That might sound simple but, given that these riders compete for different trade teams with different priorities in different places all over the world for most of the year, creating any form of team spirit was no mean feat.

The target was to win the 2011 edition of the one-day elite men's road race, which was to take place in Copenhagen. The 266km course involved a 28km ride out from the city centre before 17 circuits of a 14km course, which in pro cycling terms was relatively flat and lent itself to a bunch sprint. With the best sprinter on the planet in the team, in reigning Tour de France green points jersey winner Mark Cavendish, it was decided that Team GB would work to control the race pace from start to finish in a bid to ensure he could keep within distance for a showdown to the line in the last 250 metres.

It was a huge ask of a cycling nation that had failed to produce a men's road World Champion for more than four decades; and in Ellingworth's opinion the riders needed firing up. Tom Simpson, the miner's son who overcame the legends of the 1960s to wear rainbow in San Sebastian in 1965, was the answer. In 2009 Ellingworth called Chris Sidwells, a cycling journalist and Simpson's nephew, to ask for help in telling the story of how one of their cycling forefathers had triumphed against all odds. Eventually he borrowed a slice of sporting history.

Ellingworth then gathered the provisional squad for the Worlds in a meeting room at a hotel in Newport during a break from training for an extraordinary presentation. He strolled over to a picture frame that had a blanket draped over it and unveiled the very silk white cycling jersey, bejewelled with rainbow stripes, that Tom Simpson had won some 44 years earlier. He pressed play on an awe-inspiring film of Tom's winning ride followed by a montage of clips of the current GB squad in action before simply asking them: "So, how do you fancy bringing one of these back here?" The seed was well and truly planted.

During the build-up to race day the British team had employed the same marginal gains approach to their preparation as was now customary. The country's cycling governing body had meanwhile fulfilled their part of the bargain with a smorgasbord of world class kit. Every detail was contemplated, from the super-streamlined bikes produced in conjunction with the McLaren F1 team to the British Cycling skinsuits and ultra-aerodynamic helmets normally used to cut down wind resistance on the track.

It culminated in a stunning sprint finish in Copenhagen, which saw Cavendish power away from Australia's Matt Goss and raise his arms in utter delight to become the first British road World Champion since Mr Tom. It was as if Simpson, with the help of his nephew two years earlier, had passed the baton on himself.

It was the latest milestone in a decade of progress, and the wins didn't stop there. The year 2012 will go down in cycling history as the year that British Cycling turned heritage, preparation and innovation into world domination. The Tour de France of that year launched an era of British supremacy in the world's most famous bike race. Team Sky's Bradley Wiggins became the first Briton to win the great race, turning Dave Brailsford's outlandish prediction of winning the race within five years into a reality two years early.

And as much as he is a world class cyclist, Wiggins is also a keen cycling historian. He saw his overall victory in 2012 as part of the broader British cycling story; from working class pioneers to marginal gains glory. Three years earlier he had been in that same group of homegrown pros in

Newport who had been inspired by the rainbow success of Tom Simpson ahead of the Copenhagen Worlds. And the Tour de France of the same year – 42 years since Tom's death – gave him the chance to pay tribute to his late compatriot as the race passed the site where he lost his life, 1.5km from the summit of Mont Ventoux. "Shed a tear today for Tom," he said after the race. "I had a little extra strength today from somewhere. Had a photo of the man on my top tube."

Fittingly, his 2012 victory also had echoes of the past. He had warmed up for the big race by winning the Criterium du Dauphine stage race in 2012. The eight-day spectacle was the scene of Brian Robinson's landmark victory in 1961, where he showed his class when he had the rare support of willing teammates. The Dauphine had only ever been won by Brits twice since – by Robert Millar in 1990 and Wiggins himself in 2011. Wiggins won the 2012 Tour by three minutes and 21 seconds from his Team Sky and GB teammate Chris Froome, who was next in line to take over the Tour mantle on behalf of the Brits.

Wiggins' year in yellow was expected to become even better when he returned to England to take part in the London Olympic Games as one of Team GB's star names. They were the Olympics and Paralympics to trump them all, costing a combined £8.77billion to stage. Fortunately, the investment yielded medals, and plenty of them. Wiggins won gold in the men's individual time trial to cap off an unforgettable year, before the rest of the British cycling team picked up almost three quarters of the gold medals available including one for Yorkshire's Ed Clancy in the team pursuit. But, to begin with, the limelight was opportunely taken by an unexpected hero: a gritty female cyclist from West Yorkshire.

The 2012 Olympics arrived with much fanfare and financial backing, prompting the confident declaration of an ambitious medal haul. Team GB officials targeted 48 medals after a four-year period in which UK Sport had poured £312 million into building on previous Olympic success in all sports. With an investment like that, the country's newspapers were twitching at the early "drought" that had left us without a single medal in the first two days of competition.

Those flames of discontent were promptly extinguished by the first star of the Games: an ultra-competitive 23-year-old cyclist from the small market town called Otley, between Leeds and the Yorkshire Dales. Lizzie Armitstead's gutsy sprint finish in the pouring rain on The Mall brought the nation to its feet. She was pipped to the gold by Dutch powerhouse Marianne Vos, but won the respect and admiration of every Briton

Lizzie Armitstead at the inaugural Ilkley Cycle Races. July 1 2014.
(Bruce Rollinson, YPN)

watching. It would prove the start of an historic career. She was declared "very, very fearless" by Dave Brailsford in the wake of a silver medal performance that summed her up perfectly.

But, like many of her cycling contemporaries, Armitstead's successful start in the sport was by no means a certainty simply because she had the ability to ride a bike quickly. As a youngster – the daughter of a teacher and an accountant who were both members of the local running club – there was no inbuilt desire to road race, nor was there a lightbulb moment that ignited a passion for churning the pedals.

Her ability as a budding athlete was never in question but two wheels did not stand out as the means with which she could excel. Her first bike was purple and fitted with a basket, and like other interests it was shelved as she focused on her first love of running. At the age of five she was chasing down teens in the annual Otley Fun Run and by the time she reached her teenage years, she was stretching her legs over 10km. As a child, it wasn't Tom Simpson or Chris Boardman she aspired to mimic, but Olympic track and field star Denise Lewis. Lizzie was an all-rounder; competing regionally in middle distance events like the 800 metres and 1,500 metres for Prince Henry's Grammar School, playing in goal for the football team, playing netball and hockey and excelling in the swimming pool.

Marianne Vos (left) pips Lizzie Armitstead to gold in the Women's Road Race on The Mall, London, on the second day of the 2012 Olympic Games. (John Giles/PA)

That all changed in 2004 when she took up an invite from her PE teacher to take part in a British Cycling Talent Team trial at school. In her mind it was nothing more than a chance to skip lessons and beat the boys but to former pro rider Jonny Clay, who was the regional British Cycling officer at the time, it was an occasion in which she shone as a diamond in the rough. Lizzie, who was 15, didn't even own a bike at the time but nevertheless smashed endurance test records. She was in the right place at the right time.

"I was never the best at anything but I would never miss a training session and I loved sport," she told me. "But I didn't take to cycling straight away. It is a complex sport to get your head around if you don't come from a cycling family."

Realising the opportunities that her natural knack for cycling could bring, her dad took up bike riding and joined Lizzie on early rides. Those outings were belated meetings with the cycling landscape that had always been just a few pedal strokes from her door. But the realities of climbing up big hills hit home on the moors and Dales of West and North Yorkshire. "It was a particularly tough place to begin," she said. "The terrain is relentless and unforgiving. In the first rides with my father I had no idea that the suffering would give me an advantage against riders from other parts of the country but, because of them, I've never had the shock of racing on climbs that I saw other riders experience; and the bad weather in races doesn't faze me. There are no easy rides and it teaches you to be tough."

It may not have been easy but the roads surrounding her hometown have proven a breeding ground for sporting success both on and off the bike. For generations pro riders from Leeds and further south have used Otley as a gateway to some of the county's most exhilarating and testing country roads. In fact, two fellow West Yorkshire sports enthusiasts, triathletes Jonny and Alistair Brownlee, were coming through the ranks at around the same time as Lizzie, leading to joint training rides with a hefty collective trophy cabinet.

Both getting out on the bike and learning the intricacies of the sport proved an education for a girl who had only ever heard of Otley Criterium and the Tour de France before saddling up. The turning point came at 16 when she won a silver medal in the 2005 Junior World Track Championships' scratch race – a straight race held over 38 laps of a velodrome. She was still playing competitive netball and hockey at the time, but her victory gave her the rush of adrenaline she craved and sparked an intrigue in the sport that blossomed as rapidly as her success. She dedicated herself to the sport under the watchful eye of British Cycling.

By 2008 she had played a starring role in helping Nicole Cooke become only the third woman – Lancashire's Mandy Jones became the second in 1982 – since Beryl Burton to win the Road World Championships women's road race. And the following year she was a senior World Champion herself after riding to gold as part of a team pursuit track setup in Poland in 2009. During the same championships Lizzie gave a glimpse of her inbuilt toughness on the bike by getting up from a painful mid-race crash in the scratch race to claim silver.

Despite her evident ability on the track, road racing appealed most to Lizzie and she took the familiar leap of faith of moving to Europe to test herself against the world's best later in 2009. It was a real examination of her will to succeed, as only the elite among female road racers were paid as full-time athletes. It was a test she relished. "I never saw it as a challenge, I saw it as an adventure," she said. "Of course trying to break through and get results to earn yourself a professional contract is very difficult, but as a 19-year-old you are doing it without pressure, you are chasing a dream. In some ways they were the best years of my career. It's only with experience and hindsight that you realise how tough it actually was."

Her determination, independence and self-confessed perfectionism is somewhat reminiscent of Burton, who was a talented Yorkshire woman who built her life around the sport that she loved. Her story is one that resonates with Lizzie as Burton actually knew her grandmother, so the story of the driven female athlete who dominated the sporting world for decades was never an untold tale as the Otley rider rose through the ranks. "She (Burton) deserves more credit than she got. Even now she is talked about as an incredible female cyclist but she should be remembered as one of Yorkshire and the country's greatest cyclists," Lizzie told me. "She sounded like a fearless competitor, the kind of racer I enjoy racing against."

Three years of living in Europe battling to earn a pro deal eventually paid off. Her stock rose dramatically through her gritty sprint to second on The Mall at London 2012, making life easier following the battles she faced during her European apprenticeship in an area of the sport that was far from flush with funding. It helped her to secure a contract with her current team, Boels-Dolmans, for the following season as one of the sport's best known athletes. She had become a face synonymous with cycling and had unknowingly helped to kick-start an interest in women's road racing in Britain.

The tough start she endured, knuckling down to make ends meet abroad, and the amount of time riders like herself need to dedicate to the sport mean Lizzie's not shy of weighing in on the gender equality debate. Since the days of Beryl Burton, when all female riders were unpaid amateurs who largely went under the radar no matter how gifted they were, prize money and sponsorship in the men's arena has far outstripped that of their female counterparts. But Lizzie is confident that things are evolving, and she is willing to do her bit to ensure it levels out sooner rather than later.

"I hope in my life time we consider both under the umbrella term 'professional cycling' rather than 'cycling' and 'women's cycling'," she told me. "There are the obvious challenges, like the of lack of media coverage and sponsorship, but this is changing slowly and there have been positive steps in introducing more races to the women's race calendar. It's important to continue to push the boundaries and fight for equality. Like Beryl, I am trying to do that by racing hard and winning."

While Lizzie was busy driving cycling forward as a figurehead for the sport in Britain, her home county was developing plans of its own to make the most of the two-wheeled feel-good factor.

GRAND DÉPART REVIVAL

British cycling's long distance relationship with the enigmatic behemoth that is the Tour de France had been a rocky 40-year affair that needed revisiting.

From the awkward first date that left a lasting negative impression in Plymouth in 1974 to the butterflies the coastal Grand Départ of '94 brought and the romance that blossomed on the Tour's circuit of London's most iconic landmarks in 2007, Britain's relationship with the most treacherous race on earth had evolved beyond recognition. British understanding of the event's magnitude had grown immensely, millions upon millions of people had embraced it on its more recent visits and the sport was transforming on home soil.

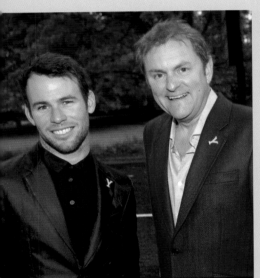

Mark Cavendish pictured with Gary Verity in Harrogate ahead of the 2014 Tour de France. (Adrian Murray, YPN)

But the country's Tour de France story needed to go full circle, it needed to go back to where it all began. The world's greatest bike race had to come to Yorkshire; or at least that was what the region's tourism boss Gary Verity had in mind. Mounting marginal gains and a thriving pool of thoroughly nurtured talent had meant winning was the norm for British cyclists by the end of the noughties. No longer was it the case that young Yorkshire riders felt that stepping on to the top step of the podium at major international races was out of reach. A huge haul of Olympic cycling medals, dozens of Cavendish Tour stage wins and a second men's British road race World Championship victory were followed up by an historic Tour de France triumph. Wiggins' charisma and performance captured the nation's hearts before Chris Froome ensured the country's new era of cycling dominance continued by claiming the yellow jersey in the 2013 Tour de France. Froome had stepped out of the shadow of being Wiggins' understudy to stake his claim as the best all-round rider in the peloton, starting the race as favourite and taking three stages on the way to a commanding overall victory by four minutes and 20 seconds.

It was this wave of excitement that needed to be harnessed further, and

Gary Verity at Buttertubs Pass ahead of the 2014 Tour de France.
(James Hardisty, YPN)

bringing the Tour back to a place that had produced the British riders who had forced their way into the centrepiece of inward-looking pro cycling was the perfect next step. Although in truth, the symbolic meaning of bringing the Tour de France to Yorkshire wasn't initially at the top of the agenda for Gary Verity; a businessman who was aiming to give the White Rose county some much-needed positive airtime amid post-recession doom and gloom.

"There was an ongoing feeling around of Manchester being some sort of Valhalla, and I found that a bit perplexing," he told me. "I did some soul searching and asked why Manchester had that and I

Dean and Russ Downing pictured with five-time Tour de France winner Bernard Hinault. (YPN)

think it was due to the Commonwealth Games in 2002. It brought a confidence to think much bigger; that's what I wanted. I wanted to make the world sit up and take note and have the people of Yorkshire have the belief to pull something off that was a bit crackers and extraordinary."

Gary describes himself as a "career chief executive". Born in Leeds, he had spent 25 years at the helm of big firms mainly in London and abroad developing what he calls "high performance teams" generally through turning around ailing companies rife with untapped potential.

But it was family trauma that brought him back home to Yorkshire, where he had owned a sheep farm in an idyllic corner of the Dales for years. His wife, Helen, was battling incurable cancer and he thought it right that they returned to their roots as she went through treatment. While tending to his wife and raising their young daughter, he was head-hunted into the role of chief executive of the Yorkshire Tourism Board, which later became known as Welcome to Yorkshire, in 2008.

Tragically, Helen passed away just a year later and through those unimaginably difficult times, Gary threw himself into his work. Spearheading the county's revival became his sole mission. The idea of bringing the Tour de France to Yorkshire actually came to him while he was having a morning shave. He thought the region's country roads and beautiful scenery would make the perfect backdrop for the televised helicopter shots taken during the biggest bike race in the world. But what he didn't realise at the time was that he had stumbled upon a gold mine of cycling heritage. With the right approach, the Tour de France could give Yorkshire the back-to-the-future fame it needed; embracing the past and plotting a course forward.

"It (the history) only really came about when we did a bit of digging," he explained. "It was an idea that was plucked out of the air but, the more you pieced it together, it became crushingly obvious that it was doable. It felt like it was meant to be."

His epiphany inspired a plan to draw on Yorkshire's cycling story and picture postcard landscapes to lure the world's most watched sporting event through an ambitious bid to host the 2014 Tour de France Grand Départ. It was a romantic idea that he hoped could reinvigorate an area he feared was at risk of becoming a "forgotten land". However, it soon became clear that it was going to be an uphill task not just to persuade the French that it could work, but also the British.

The UK Government had already made its mind up on what it wanted. Whitehall was well behind the idea of bringing the Tour back to the UK following the success of the 2007 visit but, with a Scottish independence referendum that it desperately wanted to win looming, it agreed to finance a bid from Edinburgh. Gary realised that it wasn't going to be a case of winning over the Government, but competing against it and the Italian city of Florence, which submitted the other significant rival proposal to ASO – the company which owns the race. "It felt like we were up against the establishment machinery at certain points," Gary told me. "And in my opinion there still is a certain animosity that we left some bad blood."

In an attempt to trump the other bids, Yorkshire promised a unique series of firsts that it hoped would tip the balance. It would host the Tour's biggest ever team presentation at Leeds' new First Direct Arena, create an annual UCI-approved Tour de Yorkshire legacy race for pros, develop a cultural arts offering through the first ever Yorkshire Festival and get people of all ages and abilities on their bikes through a scheme called Cycle Yorkshire. The Grand Départ itself would comprise of three Tour stages including two in the White Rose and one that would again visit the capital. It was a grand plan to say the least.

Sensing his opportunity, Verity then went 'all-in' to win the hearts of an organising body more au fait with snow-capped Alpine mountain ranges and Parisian grandeur than Dales vistas and Sheffield steelworks. Yorkshire's dormant Tour de France story needed to be told, the remote treasures of the county's landscape needed to be seen and the desire to do something different needed to be illustrated one way or another. First, the symbol of Yorkshire's Tour was born when Gary mowed and painted a huge Y into the lawn outside his farmhouse; it was the first thing ASO's top dogs saw when they were flown in by a helicopter he had borrowed for the day. A reception, crammed with Yorkshire pudding canapes and local lager was followed by a chauffeur-driven tour of Middleham Castle, Swinton Park and Harewood House in two stretch limos. A Michelin-starred local chef then laid on a feast for the likes of Tour race director Christian Prudhomme before the star of the show and guest of honour was unveiled. "They dragged me up out of a grave somewhere and presented me all over the place," Brian Robinson, who had been content living under the radar for half a century, told me with a smile. "I must admit I enjoyed it though – and it's still going on." The stops were well and truly pulled out, and the icing on the cake proved to be the screening of a promotional film in Leeds' Millennium Square detailing Yorkshire's bid, ending with a personal plea from superstar sprinter Mark Cavendish – a man with connections to the county that was his mother's home.

The battle was on with the Government's preferred Edinburgh bid, which

Mark Cavendish leads the cyclists down the Headrow in Leeds at the start of the 2014 Tour de France. July 5 2014. (Simon Hulme, YPN)

had been promised £10 million of funding. But, dazzled by Verity's spectacular show and unique set of promises, ASO took a massive gamble by signing on the dotted line with Welcome to Yorkshire in late 2012. The funding arrangements at the time were loose and incomplete, and the White Rose had never hosted anything near an event of this scale. Ministers in Whitehall were seething. The battle had been won but the war had just begun.

"Without the attention to detail we would never have had the Grand Départ," Gary told me. "It was an audacious bid from a place the French had never really heard of. We had to do a lot of explaining as to why it even needed to be on the longlist and it was really important to immerse ourselves in the history. Christian Prudhomme always says 'you understand the Tour'."

The red-faced Culture Minister Hugh Robertson sheepishly told the Commons soon after that, despite pressure from fellow MPs, Government would provide no direct funds to Yorkshire's Grand Départ. Minutes from a meeting of bosses of UK Sport, VisitEngland and the Department of Culture, Media and Sport – released to the *Yorkshire Post* through the Freedom of Information Act – later laid bare the disquiet in the chambers of Government in March 2013. Officials from UK Sport had urged the Government not to issue Yorkshire public money, describing the project as "very high risk", while casting doubts over Welcome to Yorkshire's ability to pull the whole thing off. They even suggested rebranding the event as "England's Grand Départ". It took a year of lobbying for UK Sport to hand over a cheque.

Yorkshire's Tour would eventually cost more than £27 million – the bill footed by regional local authorities (£11m), Transport for London (£6m) and UK Sport (£10m) – at a time of shrinking public spending. It was a tight, almost experimental budget for an event of unprecedented scale, especially when you consider the London Olympics cost a whopping £8.77billion.

Sir Rodney Walker, a former boss of UK Sport who is from Wakefield, was appointed chair of the event's organising body – the not-so-catchily titled TDFHUB2014 Ltd – and saw the rift from both sides. He told me after the 2014 Tour that the Culture Minister and his successor at UK Sport were enraged by ASO's decision. "Gary's intervention was to say the least unwelcome and my first real interaction was when my successor and chair of UK Sport said 'do you know that man? Can you tell him to back off?'" Sir Rodney said. "I didn't even bother asking. I think I also said 'do not underestimate his ability to win'."

Gary Verity is a charismatic charmer with the gift of the gab. In fact, I'd describe him as a journalist's dream; the perfect interviewee. You will rarely read an article in which he is quoted that is shy of a killer soundbite or a rare titbit to give the right people at the right time the key information that will ensure his cause gets optimum coverage. But beneath the smooth talking facade lies a driven and determined businessman, proud of where he comes from, who wants nothing more than to succeed. And the blatant lack of Government confidence or backing will no doubt have spurred him on. Sir Rodney was right.

Gary's resolve was tested to its limits during the trials and tribulations of the race's long build-up but his enthusiasm and the looming sense of occasion led him to do everything in his power to make it a success. With the cash in place, it was all systems go at Welcome to Yorkshire. Announcement after announcement, the Leeds-based agency was attacking the Grand Départ from all sides in a bid to harness public support.

Cycling's biggest names were due to ride, including home favourites Cavendish and reigning champion Froome, and the two Yorkshire stage routes were set out with help from two brothers who encapsulated the battle with adversity that generations of the region's riders had faced. Russ and Dean Downing would not ride the Tour de France during their careers but if the race was coming through their home county, they wanted to play a part – as did a whole host of Yorkshire's cycling great and good in a bid to help raise its profile in the region. The brothers advised the race organisers on possible routes, informed them about what to expect and tested the roads themselves. Their help was so fundamental that they attended the unveiling of the stage routes in Paris. "Everybody thinks it's brilliant, but it's absolutely bonkers to get the biggest races in the world on our doorstep," Russ told me. "Now it's the norm. I was privileged to work with Welcome to Yorkshire in bringing it here. It would have been nice to have ridden, but that's life."

Stage one would take an undulating 123-mile path from Leeds Town Hall to Harrogate, with the official timed start beginning outside the stately home Harewood House. Riders would carve through the Wharfe Valley, head to Skipton and tackle three categorised climbs in the stunning Yorkshire Dales including the scenic Buttertubs Pass before finishing on The Stray in Harrogate. The second stage included nine categorised climbs as it snaked west from York to Bolton Abbey and then down through Bronte Country, Calderdale and Huddersfield before arriving in Sheffield. Among the climbs was Holme Moss – Brian Robinson's old stomping ground.

Chris Froome pictured at the start of the first stage of the Tour de France in Leeds. July 5 2014. (Bruce Rollinson, YPN)

The peloton passes through West Tanfield during stage one of the 2014 Tour de France. July 5 2014. (Scott Merrylees, YPN)

The Tour de France peloton descends from the summit of Buttertubs Pass on stage one of the 2014 Tour de France. July 5 2014. (Tony Johnson, YPN)

Fans scale the Holme Moss climb before the start of stage two of the 2014 Tour de France. July 6 2014. (Simon Hulme, YPN)

It was at the 100 days to go point that the magnitude of what was set to arrive in Yorkshire really hit home. Up until then there had been growing numbers of cyclists on the roads, the first few decorative bikes sprayed yellow put out on display along the route and signs that the red and white polka dot, green and white of the remaining Tour jerseys would be embraced as the region's new adopted colour scheme. But Welcome to Yorkshire's annual business conference, this time a pre-Grand Départ showcase called Y14, gave an indication of the glamour and scale of what was to come. Five-time Tour de France winner Bernard Hinault and Deputy Prime Minister Nick Clegg were in attendance as the legacy race, the Yorkshire Festival arts programme of 2,225 events, the official Grand Départ theme song and details of the Tour's biggest ever team presentation both raised eyebrows and heartrates. There was so much to come. Verity's publicity machine was rolling on at pace and Yorkshire was soaking it all up.

In the weeks ahead residents in practically every town, village and city situated along the routes set about transforming their neighbourhoods by giving them a lick of paint and creating eye-catching displays as they awaited the arrival of both the world's greatest riders and thousands of cycling fans from all over the world. From the huge Tour-themed pieces of 'land art' designed to be seen from helicopter-mounted TV cameras to the redecoration of Bank View Café in Langsett to make it permanently polka dot, it was becoming clear that something special was about to happen.

In the week leading up to the Tour, the world's media arrived in Yorkshire ahead of the start of stage one. Journalists who have followed the great race all over Europe were ushered into a huge temporary media centre across the road from the offices of the *Yorkshire Post* where I was working at the time. All of a sudden, the city was awash with team cars, TV satellite trucks and accents and dialects from all over the globe. It had become the nerve centre for everything Le Tour.

One of the first assignments for reporters was the Tour de France team presentation. They are usually, by all accounts, pretty dull affairs where the team line-ups are formally paraded in front of hardcore cycling fans in their race kit. Verity's Yorkshire operation was never going to follow suit. Instead, the riders were told to hop on their bikes and ride through Leeds to the city's brand new 13,000-seat First Direct Arena for a glitzy showcase that was gobbled up by locals. They lined the streets to get a glimpse of the likes of Chris Froome as he gently rolled his way to the arena. It was a far cry from the understated yet picturesque display put on in Corsica a year earlier. Yorkshire's effort was over the top and unprecedented; and we still had two

Buttertubs Pass, Hawes – Heading north from Hawes takes you over this almighty ridge visited by the 2014 Tour de France. It's a 5km hill that has a 17 per cent rise at its steepest and continues to step up towards the summit before it evens out. It can also be tackled from Thwaite in the north.

days until the race was due to start.

As the hours rolled by more and more details about exactly what we could expect from the county's debut Grand Départ emerged. The celebrated commercial circus that is the Tour's publicity caravan was to roll from Leeds' ceremonial start line on The Headrow hours before the pros – as was expected – but then the riders would meet none other than Prince Harry and the Duke and Duchess of Cambridge at Harewood House. A Red Arrows flypast was also organised before the teams were waved off for the timed section of the first stage. It would prove a stunning start to a spectacular weekend.

Leeds was a hive of activity on the morning of stage one. The city was on lockdown and roads a stone's throw from the route were closed. Meanwhile dozens of expectant towns and villages in the Dales and those around and including Harrogate were gearing up for what was going to be an event that would be synonymous with them for years to come. Yellow bikes signalled every turn, a total of 23,000 knitted jerseys were hung as bunting in villages across the region, and would-be Banksys daubed playful cycling graffiti on the roads saying everything from 'Ey Up TDF' and 'Va Va Froome' to 'Go Cav' and 'Where's Wiggo?' in a tongue-in-cheek nod to the traditions of the continent.

Families – people who had never even considered watching, never mind attending, a pro bike race before – had camped out overnight in remote locations across Yorkshire ahead of the lengthy road closures in a bid to get a passing glimpse of the peloton. They stood 10-deep in places alongside hardcore cycling fans, waving flags and screaming their support. The excitement was palpable.

The pomp and ceremony of stage one was enough to rival any Grand Départ to have gone before. The riders, led out by Mark Cavendish, lined up on The Headrow in the city centre – outside the same Leeds Town Hall that was at the centre of an energy-charged firework display the night Yorkshire's Tour destiny was announced 18 months earlier. The Omega Pharma-Quickstep sprinter had been cleverly adopted by Verity's team as the hometown hero because of his tenuous link to Harrogate, but nobody questioned the idea of a fairytale victory. Could a British rider win a Tour stage on home turf? Cavendish certainly hoped so, and looked in high spirits rolling through Leeds during the leisurely 17.5km ride out to the official start line at Harewood House. The timed race might not yet have been underway but that didn't stop hundreds of thousands of people storming Leeds to celebrate its day in the sun.

The Royals awaited the peloton at Harewood, along with thousands more fans who had snapped up a place at one of the weekend's packed spectator hubs. Kate, William and Harry shook hands with the riders about to embark on a three-week 3,700km ordeal before the Red Arrows flew by. The stage was set.

Shortly after the 190km first stage officially got underway, veteran Jens Voigt was joined by Nicolas Edet and Benoit Jarrier in an early break that made up more than three minutes on the rest of the pack. The sun-soaked Saturday saw the main peloton give chase, swooping through Wharfedale, into Skipton and on through the Dales.

The first major climb was Kidstones Pass. The fact that it was only termed a meagre category four climb – rankings go from four, being the easiest, to one, being very hard, and above that are hills deemed 'hors catégorie' or 'beyond categorisation' – illustrated to cycling fans just how much of an uphill task awaited the world's best road racers when they reached the continent. On the climb, the crowds were keen to show their appreciation for the efforts of the riders, getting close, at times almost too close, by patting their heroes on the back in scenes reminiscent of the Tour's iconic mountain ascents.

The three-man breakaway soon fractured when Voigt attacked, picking up sprint points in the process at Newbiggin, before stretching his lead to five minutes. He continued to front the race through the bunting bedecked villages of Bainbridge and Hawes before he gritted his teeth and tackled Buttertubs Pass. The popular climb is a jewel of a hill in the Dales that takes 4.5km to cover at an average gradient of nearly seven per cent. It's not for the feint-hearted but still only ranks as a category three in comparison with 'hors catégorie' Tour mountains like the Galibier, Tourmalet and L'Alpe d'Huez. Voigt and the following riders were greeted like heroes by thousands who had dressed up and camped out along the remote staggered incline of one of the county's most iconic roads. It was a beautiful welcome made all the more spectacular by the overhead shots captured by the Tour's choppers that were hovering on high.

Among the crowds of spectators were scores of former Yorkshire pros, who could barely believe their eyes. Sid Barras, the man who had always aspired to emulate Tour legends like Tom Simpson before his European dream was crushed in the 1970s, camped out with his family to see the riders fly down the descent from Buttertubs. "I stood at the bottom and my mind, while I was waiting there, went back 50-odd years to riding over the Buttertubs on a fixed gear when I was 15 years old. I had a Bianchi," he remembered. "It

Yellow jersey holder Marcel Kittel (right) passes York Minster with the peloton on the second day of the 2014 Tour de France. (Jonathan Gawthorpe, YPN)

was a 120-mile round trip at 14 or 15 years old. I thought 'wow, I was stood there in 1962 and now the Tour de France is coming down'. It was incredible."

Piercing the cheers of the roadside spectators was Voigt, who clung on to the lead through Thwaite and Muker and up to the summit of the final climb of the day, Grinton Moor, which proved another reminder of the strength of Yorkshire's support. His valiant charge was eventually snuffed out by the peloton as it raced towards the finale on Harrogate's Stray. And, as the lead riders flashed through West Tanfield and Ripon, it was clear that stage one would end in a bunch sprint.

The peloton was eating up the tarmac through Ripley and, as the riders entered the final kilometre, Yorkshire's hopes of a Cavendish win turbocharged the atmosphere. The fairytale was on. Fabian Cancellara attacked to open a small gap on the field, with the uphill sprint finish in sight, before Cavendish looked to make his move. But, with riders jostling for space looking for the perfect line, he collided with Simon Gerrans. An almighty crash brought three riders down including Cavendish, dislocating his shoulder and rendering his entire Tour over just 200 metres from the stage one finish line. His rival Marcel Kittel pounced on his misfortune and stormed

The peloton makes its way up Haworth's Main Street during the second stage of the Tour de France 2014. July 6 2014. (Bruce Rollinson, YPN)

a head-to-head sprint with Peter Sagan to take the yellow jersey in a breathless finish to a stunning stage.

As the dust settled on stage one, it was all hands to the pump to ensure the historic city of York and its busy racecourse were ready for the start of stage two. A short tour of the medieval city centre provided ample picture opportunities before the timed race got underway near Upper Poppleton and the peloton powered west along the A59 towards Knaresborough.

A breakaway formed almost straight away, with seven riders making their point early on while the rest joined forces for a relatively flat calm before the storm. The German Kittel, majestic in yellow, coasted through the North Yorkshire villages that were still reeling from the events of yesterday's race. He was even heard saying "what a beautiful day" at one point during the ride, although he had a slight hiccup when he came off his bike while chasing the pack after a comfort break.

Harrogate, still recovering from stage one, was briefly revisited as the Tour juggernaut ploughed on towards the short climb at Blubberhouses where fans had set up shop on the opposing cliffs to get a snapshot of the riders in the bigger picture of the Yorkshire landscape. The competitors then swooped through Keighley and up Haworth's famous cobbled Main Street; the road so narrow that fans perched on steps waving their White Rose flags to cheer on the pros. The Oxenhope Moor hill was up next and measuring at 3.1km in distance and more than six per cent in gradient, it proved a pretty sound introduction to the climbs that were to come. The early leaders, nevertheless, kept a two-minute lead on the peloton as they headed through Hebden Bridge.

The breakaway kept up a decent gap as it crossed the summits of the Ripponden and Greetland climbs before the peloton finally reeled it in during the colourful tow through Huddersfield. Holme Moss would be the next test of strength but it looked almost unrecognisable. The category two epic was lined with fans hoping to get extra close to their heroes; and get close they did, leaving only a rabbit warren of a pathway to the top of one of the county's best-known cycling hills. Tommy Voeckler launched his attack there and stormed more than a minute ahead of the peloton. Meanwhile not even the cheering crowds were enough to provide the man in yellow, Kittel, with the impetus to stay with the leaders as he dropped back through the field. The sprinter's problems were confounded when he punctured soon after.

A breath-taking descent and scenic ride along Woodhead Pass provided some welcome relief, punctuated by the blink-and-you'll-miss-it dart past the polka dot Bank View Café in Langsett. But the relentless climbing was beginning to take its toll on more than just Kittel as the field was led over the day's sixth ascent at Midhopestones. By this time the lead group had swallowed up Voeckler and had been whittled down to less than 30 riders. Chris Froome's Team Sky decided to take advantage, moving to the front on the approach to Sheffield via the climb at Bradfield and then the short but steep nine per cent hill at Oughtibridge.

But Pierre Rolland and Jean-Christophe Peraud had different ideas, sneaking off before being hauled back with 8km to go. The race was on to the final climb, the Jenkin Road ramp in Sheffield that was less than a kilometre in length but almost 11 per cent in gradient; it was going to sting the legs, that was for sure. Two-time Tour winner Alberto Contador hit the front on the final hill as Froome was roared on by the vibrant home crowd alongside the Italian Vincenzo Nibali. Froome sensed victory and attacked near the top, crossing the summit first before Jakob Fuglsang took off on the descent at Meadowhall, and attack followed attack. It was anyone's race. With 2km to go Nibali set off like a rocket, leaving the field aside from the chasing duo of Richie Porte and Peter Sagan, but they couldn't catch him. Nibali – racing in the red, white and green of his native Italy – had sprung a surprise and taken stage two and the yellow jersey.

Nibali might have impressed in victory but the true shock and awe had been reserved for Yorkshire. All told, more than 3.3 million people lined the county's roads to welcome the Tour de France. The big wigs behind the continent's quirky, time-honoured tradition had thrown the dice by entrusting their prized asset with the White Rose and it had paid off. Huge swathes of the local population, many new to cycling, quite literally opened their doors to the world on those two days in Yorkshire. The witty displays, tongue-in-cheek road markings, funny costumes, banners, flags and bunting were the result of the region's hard work and all of that was captured by cameras that beamed those spine-tingling pictures to a global audience of hundreds of millions. The viewers, riders and even the Tour organisers were taken aback; race director Christian Prudhomme dubbed the county "sexy Yorkshire" following the Grand Départ. His words might have been lost in translation a little but Yorkshire's role at cycling's top table was finally assured.

When asked what his strongest memory of that weekend was, Gary Verity told me: "It was how it united Yorkshire. We've seen how divided we can be but everybody came together for the Tour de France. Communities and different organisations who all worked in their own silos decided to reach out to each other; and that spirit of working together has continued."

CLASSIC CLIMBS

Holme Moss, Holmfirth – This iconic Yorkshire climb featured during stage two of the 2014 Tour and is a favourite of Brian Robinson, who used to hold its hill climb record. Leaving Holmfirth, the A6024 starts to rise just past Holme and continues to do so over more than 2km with an unwavering 12 per cent gradient.

Fans cheer on the cyclists as they tackle the Holme Moss climb during stage two of the 2014 Tour de France. July 6 2014. (Simon Hulme, YPN)

Statistics released after Nibali crossed the line in South Yorkshire, before ultimately winning his first Tour, suggest the regional economy also benefitted to the tune of £102 million over the two days. But most importantly, the ecstasy and excitement of Yorkshire's Grand Départ renewed interest in a sport ingrained in the county's sporting DNA. The Holme Moss climb that Brian Robinson once held the record for, the winding Dales roads that Beryl Burton and Barry Hoban pounded along throughout their careers and those South Yorkshire epics that Tom Simpson will no doubt have trained long and hard on were brought back to life.

Echoes of the past offered an exciting hope for the future and much of that was down to the foresight and drive of Gary Verity, who was later knighted for his efforts. The Tour conveniently met the criteria for Welcome to Yorkshire's plan to get people across the world talking about the White Rose. But what they had stumbled upon was an event that could revitalise Yorkshire folk and give due credit to the forefathers of British cycling success, whose stories – in the era of post-millennial marginal gains – had been consigned to the history books. This was a Tour that both owed much to the drive of the White Rose's cycling greats and expanded upon their legacies.

Former Tour de France winner Alberto Contador (centre) tackles the Holme Moss climb during stage two of the 2014 Tour de France. July 6 2014. (Simon Hulme, YPN)

Jenkin Road, Wincobank, Sheffield – *Famed for its role as the last hill of the 2014 Grand Départ's second stage, this short 1km climb begins after a sharp turn and then hits a 25 per cent gradient section as the road anchors left.*

The peloton climbs the steepest part of Jenkin Road in Sheffield towards the end of the second stage. (Tony Johnson, YPN)

TAKING THE NEXT STEP

Would Yorkshire's Grand Départ become an impressive footnote in the country's sporting history books? Not if Sir Gary Verity had anything to do with it.

The Tour de France was an inspired target for a man determined to showcase his home county to the world but throughout the build-up to the region's day in the sun it was repeatedly stressed that this was the beginning of something big; not the climax in a one-off adventure. A legacy was central to the vision.

Plans for an annual 'Tour de Yorkshire' were unveiled in the weeks leading up to the 2014 Tour. The great race's owners ASO signed a three-year deal with Welcome to Yorkshire to stage it. It would initially be a three-day event spread over the May bank holiday weekend every year and, crucially, it would be recognised as part of the UCI Europe Tour as a 2.1 event. The ranking made it an attractive proposition to some of cycling's biggest teams, if the promise of euphoric Yorkshire crowds was not enough. And with cycling proving a growing market in the UK and Yorkshire in particular, it was hoped big name sponsors would get the exposure they desired in a race around the White Rose. The addition of a mass 'sportive' ride for amateurs during the event proved another selling point. The Tour de Yorkshire was a no-brainer.

Logistically it made sense but the challenge of following up the world's most prestigious bike race on a budget that wasn't bolstered by central Government was no mean feat. It would rely on contributions from the local councils which bid to become start or finish points – often paying a few hundred thousand pounds to host their section of the race – and sponsorship from private companies. It needed to be put on at a fraction of the £27 million of its predecessor. Rightly, from the start the viewing public was warned it would "not be on the same scale" as the Tour de France, but that didn't stop people embracing it. "It wasn't a come down from the Tour," Sir Gary told me. "It was our race, whereas we borrowed somebody else's during the Tour de France. With the Tour de Yorkshire we're able to impose our personality on it even more and we've seen that on the routes we've chosen so far."

Arguably, the only thing missing from the 2014 Grand Départ was a British stage victory, and fans were hoping to see that redressed. The team line-ups boosted hopes of a GB home win with one of the biggest names in pro cycling. Sir Bradley Wiggins, who was knighted in 2013, was to appear as

Sir Bradley Wiggins lines up on the start line for the third stage of the 2015 Tour de Yorkshire in Wakefield. (YPN)

part of his own Team Wiggins, while the start list was also littered with 12 Yorkshire names including Ben Swift, Russ Downing, Ed Clancy and Tom Barras, whose appearance would be his pro cycling swansong. A whole host of top continental pros also got behind it, including the winner of stage one of the 2014 Tour, Marcel Kittel.

The inaugural Tour de Yorkshire charted a new, broader course through the county, exploring the Yorkshire coast and North York Moors that also have their fair share of cycling history. The same roads that were taken in by the likes of Barry Hoban and his clubmates the best part of half a century before would help to form the 174km first stage from Bridlington to Scarborough. The route featured four climbs including the 10 per cent gradient ramp out of Robin Hood's Bay.

Ed Clancy at the start in Wakefield of stage three of the 2015 Tour de Yorkshire. May 3 2015.
(Bruce Rollinson, YPN)

Riders race through Newmillerdam during stage three of the 2015 Tour de Yorkshire. May 3 2015. (YPN)

The weather held out for the launch of the stage on Bridlington's South Marine Drive although the looming grey clouds above soon played their part. The North Yorkshire communities that missed the Tour the year prior were galvanised by having their own piece of the race's legacy and gave signature welcomes to the 144-rider strong peloton. For Ben Swift, who had missed out on the 2014 Tour, taking in a unique Yorkshire welcome in the midst of a top international bike race was something he never thought he'd get to experience as a professional. And although he crashed out on a slippery descent at Grosmont on stage one, the memories of those opening sections of the race are still vivid. "As a kid growing up, I never expected to see the Tour de France on my home roads let alone a race that's really big and becoming a big thing," he explained. "I had a bad experience that first year but the level of support we got in the middle of nowhere was just amazing. I remember turning around to my teammates at one point and asking 'what did you say?' – thinking the people shouting me were riders. It was unbelievable."

The German sprinter Kittel also withdrew after falling ill as the riders navigated the tight roads and coastal climbs. The crucial move came 40km from the line as the race passed through Whitby when a 15-man break formed that was ground down to just five riders at Robin Hood's Bay. Despite numerous attacks, the group stayed together to the end and Team Sky's Lars Petter Nordhaug sprinted to victory.

Stage two from Selby Abbey to York would explore the Wolds and Humberside through to York along a relatively flat 174km course. Following a leisurely tour around Selby town centre, the timed race started near Market Weighton. An early break again formed, with eight riders building a seven-minute lead on the rest of the field. The group's lead was cut thanks to hard chasing by Team Sky and IAM Cycling and, as the race entered York city centre, the last members of the splinter group were hunted down. Greg Van Avermaet attacked with less than 1km to go and looked set to secure the win before being caught by Moreno Hofland, who claimed the stage.

Day two also featured a women's race, but it attracted criticism from the off. Lizzie Armitstead was vocal about the fact it was designed effectively as a criterium circuit race around York city centre rather than a challenging road race. She opted out, arguing that the event should take place over three days like the men's race. It was a blow to the inaugural Tour but a top field of female riders got involved regardless, including 11-time Paralympic cycling champion Dame Sarah Storey and Chris Walker's daughter Jessie. A field of 98 women contested the 80km race, which ended in a breathless sprint victory by Louise Mahé.

The men revisited some of the same roads that the Tour de France graced a year earlier during stage three; only in the opposite direction. They were to race from Wakefield to Barnsley, before heading to Ripponden, Hebden Bridge and Haworth through Wharfedale to Leeds' Roundhay Park. Six gruelling climbs awaited including Ilkley's Cow and Calf, which was visited by the Tour of Britain in 2004.

But the Tour de Yorkshire's most challenging stage yet didn't just stand in the way of the pros. Around 6,000 amateurs took part in the first Tour de Yorkshire Ride sportive along a similar route in the driving rain hours before the stars. It may have proven a bit of a wash-out weather-wise but in terms of participation and feel-good factor it added another stunning facet to the county's latest sporting spectacle. It was even led out by retired professional and Dave Rayner Fund beneficiary, David Millar.

As the amateurs filtered into Roundhay Park to collect their finishing medals, a six-man breakaway had formed among the pros on the outskirts of Wakefield. It eventually built a five-minute lead on the peloton. The brave escapees were cheered on like heroes by the biggest crowd of the Tour weekend so far, with around 750,000 people willing them along roads that had been engulfed by the Tour de France less than a year earlier. The break was reeled in before the crucial jump by BMC's Ben Hermans came 11km from the race's climax in Leeds' Roundhay Park. The finish line crowds, bolstered by thousands of accomplished amateurs, roared the Belgian to victory.

Lars Petter Nordhaug of Team Sky took the race overall but the absence of a home victor didn't detract from what was an incredible start to Yorkshire's own Tour. An estimated 1.2 million spectators took to the streets in support of the race including none other than the Prime Minister David Cameron, who had popped up in Addingham, near Ilkley, to catch a glimpse of stage three.

For some of the riders, it was the pinnacle of their careers. Tom Barras' pro cycling mission had allowed him to see both the depressing lows and jubilant highs of road racing in Britain. Forced abroad as an aspiring pro, he battled for survival on the continent before riding the wave of cycling optimism in a domestic scene buoyed by Olympic success. Aged 36 and riding for the Yorkshire-based NFTO team, his knowledge of the race route was utilised as he worked for his team's sprinter as a domestique in 2015. It was a race he will never forget.

2015 Road Race
World Champion
Lizzie Armitstead.
(Bruce Rollinson, YPN)

Tour de Yorkshire passes through Beverley during stage two of the 2015 Tour de Yorkshire. May 2 2015. (YPN)

World Champion Lizzie Armitstead meets fans after the Tour de Yorkshire Women's Race from Otley to Doncaster, Saturday 30th April 2016. (Chris Etchells, YPN)

"It was basically three days of the Tour de France in Yorkshire," Barras, who stepped off the bike to become sporting director at NFTO at the end of that season, told me. "I rode the route of every stage three times and I knew every inch of it. To ride literally past my own house and past Otley Chevin at the front of the bunch was like ending on a high. I rode up through the crowd of my friends clapping and cheering and I thought 'this is mega'. The crowds were five deep, it was unbelievable. This Yorkshire legacy thing just wasn't around when I was growing up; I'm so glad I got a piece of that."

For Yorkshire's growing number of cycling fans, it was perfect pre-Tour de France viewing. Vincenzo Nibali's 2014 Tour win broke Britain's two-year occupation of the great race's yellow jersey before classy Chris Froome, who crashed out of the 2014 race suffering a broken hand and wrist, reinstated his dominance of elite stage races by claiming the 2015 edition.

The year also proved an unforgettable one for Lizzie Armitstead. The Road Race World Championship title is the most coveted in women's cycling and, at 26, she felt in prime position to bring it home. Without a major Grand Tour as such, women's cycling largely centres around smaller stage races and big one-day road races – the pinnacle being the annual Worlds and the Olympic road race that comes around every four years. Lizzie was in peerless form throughout 2015, claiming the British national road race title and the UCI Women's Road World Cup series. But the dream was to win the World Championship road race. By claiming the rainbow jersey, she would become only the fourth British female road race World Champion. She would be writing her name alongside the great Beryl Burton in the history books.

The 2015 Worlds took place in September over a 130km course that comprised of eight laps of a city centre circuit in Richmond, Virginia, in the USA. Planning for it had started months earlier in June when Lizzie, who tailored her entire year around the event, practiced the route while in America for a different race. It became clear then that she would need to build the power and endurance to hold back enough energy for the final hill on the course before blasting past the opposition in a sprint to the line.

By the time the race came around, she was in the shape of her life and among the favourites. But well aware of the magnitude of the occasion she kept to her plan of ensuring her gung-ho tendencies, sparked by a natural power and competitive nature, were reigned in. Lizzie controlled the race from the front.

Holding her nerve in the face of a nine-woman breakaway that escaped 20km from the line, she led the charge that gradually reeled in the rival

Lars Petter Nordhaug wins the opening stage at the 2015 Tour de Yorkshire in Scarborough. May 1 2015.
(Bruce Rollinson, YPN)

CLASSIC CLIMBS

Cow and Calf, Ilkley – This climb features stunning rock faces to the right and even more breathtaking views of the Wharfe Valley to the left. It's been visited by the Tour of Britain and Tour de Yorkshire, and lasts about 2km. The steady 12 per cent bank is only broken up by a cattle grid in the middle.

The peloton of the Tour de Yorkshire makes its way through the crowds on the Cow and Calf in Ilkley on stage three on May 3 2015. (Tony Johnson) group to set up the sprint finish that she had played out in her mind hundreds of times before. Lizzie powered up the final climb and waited for someone to bolt. Anna Van der Breggen, of Holland, took the bait and hit top gear, prompting Lizzie to slot in behind and ramp up the pace. With metres to the line, the Brit edged past and refused to let go of the lead. She threw absolutely everything she had into it, crossing the line in tears. Lizzie had done it; she was World Champion.

She had made history and earned the admiration of those before her. Both her own cycling journey and that of the lottery-funded women's side of the sport had reached the perfect climax. "Lizzie is wonderful. She got an opportunity and she grasped it," Denise Burton-Cole told me. "We were given an opportunity but we were on our own. They were different times. In my day, we didn't have coaches and I don't think my mother would have listened anyway to be honest. It's so, so different. I don't think people who are young now could imagine it but everybody was in the same boat. It's great that things have evolved."

And Yorkshire's reigning World Champion enjoyed her well-earned stint in rainbow during an extra special homecoming. She took part in the 2016 Tour de Yorkshire. Her criticism of the 2015 edition led race organisers, to their credit, to seek her thoughts on how to make a success of it. She worked with them to create an engaging one-day road race that would exactly mirror the course the men would take – 136.5km from Lizzie's home town of Otley to Doncaster via three classified climbs. Another significant step in the journey to parity was the inclusion of a £15,000 prize for the winner, making it the most lucrative race in the women's cycling calendar. "I had goose bumps starting as World Champion in Otley," she told me. "It was a privilege and something I'll never forget. It's important that when we are given opportunities to race with the equivalent exposure as the men that we can showcase our sport; that means we need full-length challenging races. Too often we do shortened versions of the men's 'flat stage' and it doesn't encourage aggressive racing and can lead to a boring few hours of TV."

But Armitstead's romantic return, resplendent in rainbow, didn't quite go to plan. The women's race was given top billing along with the rest of the Tour de Yorkshire, receiving a slot on ITV4 and Eurosport. But a transmission issue meant her attack that burst the race into life at Conisbrough Castle was seen only by the roadside fans and not the global audience of TV viewers. She was eventually brought back to the group and the bunch sprint was taken by Kirsten Wild.

The men's race again took place over three days, and once more the stars aligned for another top draw spectacle. Sir Bradley Wiggins returned to race for the second year in succession, as did Russ Downing, while top teams including BMC and Team Sky came back for more; starting with a relatively flat 185km first stage from Beverley to Settle. Unfortunately, it wasn't blessed with the largely bright and dry weather of the years prior; a point highlighted by a crash within the first kilometre that caused Wiggins to abandon. Nevertheless, the crowds turned out in their thousands and gave a typically vibrant welcome to the riders as the peloton weaved through the towns and villages leading to the Dales. The Dutchman Dylan Groenewegen eventually won the stage from pre-race favourite Caleb Ewan during a tense sprint finish that was witnessed by a blue and yellow sea of spectators.

Otley's residents didn't seem too bothered about the bad weather on day two. A typically chipper reception saw one butcher in the town dress his window with a 'Sir Bradley Piggins' display that summed up the smiles as the Saturday stage got underway. The day's racing was fast-paced and included three tricky climbs between Otley and Doncaster but it was a small, flat detour south before the finish that took the headlines. Sir Gary, constant in his message, explained: "We've got to chart our history and heritage and learn from it and that's really important."

Almost 50 years after his death, the Tour de Yorkshire poignantly passed through Tom Simpson's adopted hometown of Harworth in a touching tribute to a tenacious rider whose personality inspired generations to get on their bikes. Without Tom and his contemporaries, it's conceivable that the Tour de Yorkshire might never have happened. Lovingly dressed with yellow bikes and Tour bunting for the visit of the race, Harworth played host to the endeavour of another cycle-mad rider who grew to relish the sport by tackling the hills of South Yorkshire. Russ Downing battled to ninth in a tight sprint finish in Doncaster that saw Team Sky's Danny van Poppel clinch the win from Groenewegen by a whisker.

Day three from Middlesbrough to Scarborough was a gruelling 198km effort littered with six hefty climbs and endless landmarks. The challenging route tackled the North York Moors; the sharp 12 per cent Sutton Bank and Grosmont climbs coming before it sped through Whitby and Robin Hood's Bay into Scarborough. The overall leaders faded on the climbs and Tommy Voeckler took advantage by racing to the stage victory and snatching the overall leader's jersey.

It had proven to be a huge success that built on the foundations of 2015, with more than two million people venturing out to the roadside as TV

The peloton climbs up Scapegoat Hill out of Slaithwaite during the Tour de Yorkshire stage three from Wakefield to Leeds. May 3 2015. (Bruce Rollinson, YPN)

viewing figures reached 11.4 million worldwide. It was bigger and better than its predecessor and, according to post-race research, gave the local economy a £60 million boost.

The British Cycling success story continued to gain pace during the summer of 2016 too. Chris Froome secured his third overall victory in the Tour de France before the Rio Olympic and Paralympic Games saw British athletes take home a huge haul of medals. Among Yorkshire's medal winners were Ed Clancy, Leeds track sprinter Katy Marchant and para cyclists Kadeena Cox and David Stone.

Cycling had gone mainstream in Britain and in Yorkshire. From being an exotic minority sport treasured by White Rose explorers, it had become an activity that the country had taken to its heart and the county took great pride in. And while London was the flagship city in terms of cycle paths, and Manchester remained the nation's track cycling hub, Yorkshire had evolved from heritage and underground passion to become the home of the road racing dream.

The spark of the Tour de France had clearly lit the touch paper on a latent pride that was deep-rooted in the region. Cycling's boom in popularity made it something that the county's people could embrace as the sport of their fathers and forefathers. Yorkshire's new-found pedigree as a road racing destination also helped to create something local people could take ownership of. Pictures of the Tour de France's visit and Tour de Yorkshire weekends serve now to urge communities on to outdo each other year-in, year-out.

Tommy Voeckler crosses the finish line on Scarborough's North Bay to win the 2016 Tour de Yorkshire overall. May 1 2016. (YPN)

The Tour de Yorkshire passes through Scarborough. (YPN)

Russ Downing climbs Sutton Bank with the peloton during stage three of the 2016 Tour de Yorkshire. May 1 2016. (Bruce Rollinson, YPN)

Scott Thwaites, from Burley-in-Wharfedale near Leeds, at the Cow and Calf Rocks above Ilkley. **January 3 2014.** (Bruce Rollinson, YPN)

THE FUTURE

Build, build, build was the mantra at the heart of Sir Gary Verity's blueprint for success for Yorkshire.

The next part of the plan to further elevate the county in the hearts and minds of world cycling chiefs is through the 2017 Tour de Yorkshire. Although it's bound by the same format, the race is hoped to provide the professional peloton with its sternest test yet.

The three days of action will start with a 173km tour of the east coast, beginning in the seaside town of Bridlington on April 28th. The race will speed through the Wolds towards a sprint section in Pocklington before hitting the first climb at Garrowby Hill, then the Goathland ramp in the North York Moors and passing through Whitby, up the Robin Hood's Bay ascent to Scarborough.

Day two will see the women's one-day race and the men's second stage take on a relatively flat 122km course from Tadcaster that loops above Harrogate at Pateley Bridge, passes over the Lofthouse climb in the Dales and speeds through Ripon to the finish in Harrogate.

To this point the routes might seem quite straight forward, but the men's event is expected to split wide open during stage three from Bradford. The 194.5km course takes in eight categorised climbs including four hefty ascents within the last 15km of

Sir Gary Verity unveils the host towns for the 2017 Tour de Yorkshire.
(Jonathan Gawthorpe, YPN)

the race. Nicknamed the 'Yorkshire Terrier' by the race organisers – although it was more aptly described as a "beast" by Sir Gary when we spoke – the stage heads north into the Dales via Ilkley, hitting Threshfield before throwing down the gauntlet with four climbs in quick succession at Silsden, Haworth Main Street, Leeming and the cobbled Shibden Wall. Riders will then pass through Halifax and Brighouse and keep going south through Holmfirth towards Sheffield, where they will face another quartet of leg burners. Climbs at Deepcar, Wigtwizzle, Ewden Height and finally Midhopestones will split the men from the boys before the finish line at Stocksbridge.

The Terrier will likely be the decider in what should be another top racing weekend, and it is hoped to build on the trend of Yorkshire Tours attracting more and more spectators every year. The roadside crowds almost doubled to two million for the 2016 edition, and the organisers hope the most testing triple header yet will warrant even more attention.

And though the evident optimism surrounding the Tour de Yorkshire might make it appear as if all is well, Sir Gary Verity has made it clear that he is far from satisfied with the status quo. The growing popularity of the race has prompted Welcome to Yorkshire to plot its course for the future by applying to expand it to become a four-day men's race and a two-day event for women. As far as they are concerned it is a win-win scenario that would give women's cycling a bigger platform and Britain an event large enough to rival the flagship Tour of Britain.

But an initial bid to expand the Tour de Yorkshire was knocked back by British Cycling in late 2015. The governing body said the existing format is part of a "balanced international racing calendar which ensures people across Britain have a chance to see world-class cycling on our roads", while also adding it was "too soon" after its launch to consider its growth.

That didn't go down well with Welcome to Yorkshire, which launched an online campaign to persuade the powers that be to review their decision. Bringing an extra day of top class men's and women's cycling to Yorkshire remains a priority. Sir Gary told me he thinks the governing body's current position is an attempt to "keep Yorkshire in its box". He explained: "It's absolutely bonkers, anybody would think it's a good idea. We would get four days of men's and two days of women's racing; and having that would help the development of women's cycling."

With the extra racing, Sir Gary said he would look to have a Yorkshire Tour comprising of two hilly stages and two flat stages, which could prove more of a draw for specialist sprinters or climbers. They could alternatively introduce a team or individual time trial into the mix for the first time.

The long-term future of the Tour de Yorkshire is another topic for debate. Welcome to Yorkshire's original three-year deal with ASO to host the race ends in 2017 but it seems the future of that agreement is quite fluid. "As long as cycling's popular, the Tour de Yorkshire will keep going," Sir Gary assured me. "I'm sure it will keep going long after I'm doing this job."

The behind-the-scenes negotiations and debates over future events seemingly never stop as the county's tourism body continues to try to thrash out a better deal for the region both nationally and internationally. Only those on the inside knew, for example, of the next ambitious vision to bring another of the sport's most prized assets to the White Rose. That plan was formulated in the wake of the 2015 Tour de Yorkshire.

Sir Gary was this time aiming to lure the annual battle for the rainbow jersey, the UCI Road World Championships, to the Yorkshire countryside. It was another audacious bid that would have once been cast aside as a mere impossibility. But Yorkshire's attempts at the extraordinary are becoming as much the norm as British riders dominating global road racing.

Over the next 18 months, Welcome to Yorkshire set about formulating a bid to rival the likes of Colombia, Germany and Canada for the right to host the 2019 edition of the championships. The bad blood left by the battle for the Grand Départ in 2014 was put to one side and the Government agreed to get involved, as did British Cycling, local authorities and other backers. Whitehall would underwrite the full cost of the event and back it with £24 million of investment, which would in part go towards funding 27 UK cycle sport facilities.

But the enormity of the task of winning over international cycling bosses should not be understated. Britain has only ever hosted the Worlds three times before – it came to Liverpool in 1922, Leicester in 1970 and Goodwood in 1982. The last time it came to Britain, Mandy Jones stunned the world with her victory in the women's road race, showing that a romantic home win is not inconceivable.

One thing that supports a Yorkshire-based Road World Championships is that the annual spectacle has a special place in the county's sporting history, with three of the region's most successful riders donning the rainbow stripes in their careers. So, if bringing the Tour de France to Yorkshire was an ode to the exploits of the likes of Brian Robinson, claiming the Worlds would pay homage to former winners Tom Simpson and Beryl Burton – not forgetting Lizzie Armitstead, who married to become Lizzie Deignan in 2016.

A feeling of déjà vu took over when the UCI announced in December of 2016 that the Worlds would indeed be held in Yorkshire in 2019 – news that led Welcome to Yorkshire to declare it a "moment in history" that reinforced the fact "we have got the scenery, the crowds, and the warm welcome" to attract the stars. It was another announcement that made the world sit up and take note. The county had won the right to host the nine-day event that features 12 races for the world's best juniors, under-23s, and elite men and women over road race and time trial disciplines. Sir Gary was coy about how the event might be structured initially but he pledged that it would touch all four corners of Yorkshire.

Scott Thwaites, from Burley-in-Wharfedale near Leeds, at the Cow and Calf Rocks above Ilkley. January 3 2014. (Bruce Rollinson, YPN)

FAVOURITE TRAINING RIDES

"There's one route I like from Rotherham through Wickersley, Tickhill, and around the backs to Clayworth and Retford and back the normal way. I'd say the Strines are my favourite climbs in Yorkshire but I use them more as a recovery ride now. We are quite lucky with the flatlands to one side and the Peaks. Going to the Peaks is a big day."

Ben Swift

Tom Barras pictured at the Otley Town Centre Road Race. June 2 2014.
(Bruce Rollinson, YPN)

He told me: "There's very strong speculation it will be centred in and around Harrogate. The finishes for each race will be there. Starts will be in the east, north, west and south but all roads will lead to Harrogate. The UCI are very wedded to their circuits so we will end up with a circuit around Harrogate but that doesn't mean to say we won't have grand loops around that. The men's race is 280km long so you could do a giant sweep of Yorkshire countryside before you get there."

And given the size of the crowds Yorkshire's big races have attracted over the last few years, he is conscious the routes will need to be big enough to accommodate millions of fans. "We need to do a big stage before the circuits," Sir Gary said. "We had a quarter of a million people in Harrogate for the Tour de France and two million came out to watch the 2016 Tour de Yorkshire, so we need to plan for that. It will be a hilly course so it will be something akin to the Tour de France but I'm not sure it will be exactly straight up for a sprint. It's tailored for somebody like Sagan as it's lumpy. We're more for a punchy rider."

That will be news to the ears of some of Yorkshire's brightest prospects as well as those who have developed a gritty all-round style through years of pounding up and down the region's undulating roads.

With that in mind, the elite women's road race could present Lizzie Deignan with a chance to score another world title. She will be approaching her 31st birthday when Yorkshire welcomes the planet's best cyclists in 2019. "I have a two-year contract with my current team Boels-Dolmans, which will take me until the end of 2018," she told me. "I had always considered retirement then until the announcement of the 2019 Yorkshire World Championships. I have always wanted to retire at the top of the sport, so I will only do Yorkshire if I believe I can win. A home World Championships would be the greatest motivation."

As Lizzie's crusade to bring the women's side of the sport to the attention of the world continues, she's likely to be challenged by the next batch of British Cycling products. The governing body's track-first approach to development is likely to mean more and more young female road racers emerge from the system and follow the Otley racer's example over the years to come.

And punchy male riders could also be in with a chance on home turf. Ben Swift, for example, is coming off the back of a disappointing spell punctuated by injuries. The period has also seen his stock lower within the progressive Team Sky but there are signs that he could actually be reaching his physical prime. Probably his two most significant results in recent years have come at the monumental Italian Classic Milan–San Remo. Swift's third in 2014 and second in the 2016 edition of the iconic 300km race, which the great Tom Simpson won back in 1964, gave a glimpse of what he can achieve with the right support, form and fitness. He has now left the Team Sky bubble for the promise of contesting more races as a team leader at the UAE Abu Dhabi setup from 2017 onwards. "This will give me the opportunity to see how good I can be in an environment where I can focus fully on myself," he told me. "Maybe I will never win a bike race again but I want to give myself the best opportunity."

If his Middle Eastern adventure works out, he hopes it could elevate him to the ultimate one-day win, potentially in his home county. "One hundred per cent I will be aiming for the Worlds in 2019," he said. "It's going to be perfect terrain for me, with no massive climbs. It's an unbelievable opportunity to have that coming to your home district. The Tour de France is one thing but the World Championships is just unbelievable. What we're going to see there is fantastic racing and the crowds will be amazing."

Adam Blythe is another Yorkshireman who is hitting his peak years, but he took another route to the likes of his childhood pal Swift. Blythe grew up in a cycling family in Dronfield, near Sheffield, and joined the Sheffield Phoenix Club as a youth, before his raw ability was picked up by British Cycling. He won national and European junior titles on the track as a 17-year-old before joining the governing body's Under-23 Academy but decided to leave the programme in 2008. He wanted to do it his way.

Blythe travelled to Belgium to gain more experience as a road racer, opting to take part in full senior races in a bid to impress pro team talent scouts. His results eventually earned him a pro deal before he moved to one of the world's biggest teams, BMC Racing. But Blythe has struggled for consistency abroad, swapping teams several times over recent years and stepping back into domestic racing with NFTO in 2014, before returning to the top table of European cycling. He was crowned British National Road Race Champion in 2016 after a tense sprint finish against Mark Cavendish, while he managed 12th in his first World Championship road race months later. He will race for Aqua Blue Sport in 2017 and is already eyeing up a place at Yorkshire's 2019 Worlds. "It's the perfect location to host the World Championships because the roads are really challenging," he said. "Years ago I never imagined the world's best riders would come here and race on the same roads I trained on, but now that's the reality."

Another prospect is Scott Thwaites, from Burley-in-Wharfedale, near Leeds. His first love was cyclo-cross and he raced for Great Britain as a youth before switching his focus to the road, where he signed as a pro with Endura Racing aged 20 in 2010. He spent three years with his first team before stepping up another level, racing some of the famous Classics and major stage races and claiming a bronze medal at the 2014 Commonwealth Games in the men's road race. His rise continued in 2016 when he made his Grand Tour debut in the Vuelta a España. He's now looking to progress further with the Dimension Data team in 2017.

Tom Pidcock, from Roundhay in Leeds, is also seemingly destined for big things. He won a stunning world title as a 17-year-old in the junior men's race at the 2017 Cyclo-cross World Championships in Luxembourg, and is already being talked about as a rider with the potential to race for one of the top pro road cycling teams. His Worlds triumph - adding to his British and European titles - is Britain's first in the event since 1992. He's also well versed in track racing and has the experience of British Cycling junior academy tuition to draw on. Whichever way he decides to go, the future looks bright.

Retired rider Tom Barras, who trains with many of the next generation, feels there are too many exciting Yorkshire riders to mention. Some of the

Adam Blythe (right) pictured during the Otley Town Centre Road Race. June 2 2014. (Bruce Rollinson, YPN)

promising talents he's worked with include Keighley's Tom Moses, ex-Team Sky rider Josh Edmondson from Leeds, Doncaster's Tom Stewart and Holmfirth's Gabriel Cullaigh, who has been making his way through the British Cycling system. He said: "The whole scene is pretty healthy; the future is bright for Yorkshire."

The very fact that we continue to produce top prospects who see winning big European titles as realistic shows just how far we've come since the days of saving up a couple of hundred pounds and throwing the dice by venturing to the continent. Those brave first steps made by the likes of Robinson, Simpson and Hoban certainly laid the foundations that turned an intrigue about what the Europeans were doing over the water into a fascination that has become an integral focus of Great Britain's sporting model.

With British Cycling's extensive talent spotting and rider nurturing infrastructure proving a production line for potential, it seems the sky's the limit. And the credit Yorkshire and the fruits of its cycling labour are increasingly being awarded for their role in broader British success is spurring the sport on to bigger and better things. Meanwhile, Yorkshire folk's never-say-die attitude to all things cycling means they are continuing to break the boundaries of what's considered conceivable for the sport on and off the bike.

God's Own Country has a lot to look forward to as far as the battle of wills on two wheels is concerned but it's still not enough; not for the likes of Sir Gary Verity at least. When I asked whether the Worlds will be the final chapter in the region's cycling boom, he told me: "Well, we've got to get the Tour de France up (to Yorkshire) again. If it's up to me that's what will happen and then my work is done. The next time will be even bigger, I can assure you." And who would put it past him?

Junior World and European cyclo-cross champion 17-year-old Tom Pidcock. 1st Febuary 2017. (Jonathan Gawthorpe, YPN)

Road racing is woven into the fabric of Yorkshire's cultural history. From the foundations of its popularity as a post-war working-class necessity to the way it gave generations the freedom to explore the White Rose's natural beauty, cycling's love story with the region is deep-rooted. Its narrative charts perseverance, tragedy, bravery, ability and a renaissance, but most of all it is one of character and passion.

Brian Robinson says there's something special in the water in these parts. But the fact he was only recognised for his sporting triumphs with a British Empire Medal in the Queen's 2017 New Year Honours list – more than 60 years after his first ground-breaking Tour de France – shows the county's cycling success is probably down to something far less mystical. Brian did not embark on a continental expedition for money or fame; he did so because he simply loved riding his bike.

A SELECTION OF YORKSHIRE'S MOST FAMOUS CLIMBS

North Yorkshire:

Fleet Moss, Hawes – This is the highest road in Yorkshire but to get to its summit you need to go south out of Hawes and take on a 5km climb out of Gayle. After the last farm, the road turns into one the region's most fearsome ascents. It ends after a 20 per cent gradient left-hander and a twisting section near the top.

Rosedale Chimney, Pickering – This beast of a climb out of Rosedale Abbey is known for being one of the toughest in Yorkshire. It lasts around 1.5km and features two sharp bends, hitting a one-in-three gradient in the middle before levelling out near the summit.

Greenhow Hill, Pateley Bridge – There are four short stretches of climbing that make up Greenhow Hill. It's a stepped 4km ascent that starts with an 18 per cent gradient ramp and then evens out over the next three sections of climbing, which finish at the sign for Greenhow village.

Buttertubs Pass, Hawes – see page 145.

Kidstones Pass, Buckden – see page 57.

Yorkshire coast:

Caper Hill, Whitby – This 1.5km climb is a straight, unflinching hill south west of Glaisdale near the Yorkshire coast. It starts with a tough one-in-four ascent before reaching a cattle grid. From there, slight kinks in the road do little to numb the pain.

Robin Hood's Bay – Starting from the village's harbour, this climb hits a 25 per cent gradient early on before levelling out and gradually ramping up once again. To complete the full 3km ascent take a left on to Thorpe Lane towards Fylingthorpe.

South Yorkshire:

Ewden Bank, Stocksbridge, Sheffield – This 1km climb forms part of the renowned Strines section of climbs between Sheffield and the Peaks. Ewden Bank is on Mortimer Road, which links the A616 and A57, and starts after Ewden Beck. A tough one-in-four left-hand bend starts the pain before a right-hander further up.

Midhopestones Bank, Sheffield – This hill forms the northern entry to the Strines and was also part of the 2014 Grand Départ's second stage. The rise lasts for about 2.5km and gets harder after a lull in the middle. Both Midhopestones and Ewden Bank will be visited by the 2017 Tour de Yorkshire.

Jenkin Road, Wincobank, Sheffield – see page 156.

West Yorkshire:

Shibden Wall, Halifax – This cobbled beast will be visited by the Tour de Yorkshire in 2017, having played host to the Milk Race in years gone by. The 25 per cent rise snakes up Lee Lane through Ovenden as your bike vibrates beneath you over what is a pretty patchy surface.

Cragg Vale, Hebden Bridge – Another climb visited by the 2014 Tour, this steady ascent lasts an incredible 9km. In fact, it's the longest continual uphill gradient in the country and it gets slightly harder the further you go. The route becomes particularly testing after you leave the village but it eventually smooths out.

Oxenhope Moor, Oxenhope – A favourite of Welcome to Yorkshire, this famous 3km rise veers left out of Oxenhope before a sharp-right turn directs you towards open moorland. The road gradually sweeps right as the gradient changes beneath you. It snakes left and right and then the hill eases.

Cow and Calf, Ilkley – see page 169.

Holme Moss, Holmfirth – see page 152.

YORKSHIRE CYCLING FANS

Andrew W Archer
Colin Armstrong
Avril Armstrong
David Arrandale
Glenda Bentley
Robert Birkinshaw
Trevor Brown
Kelman Cowie
Ronald Creighgon
Charlie Cromack
Albert Davies
Craig Dobson
Elizabeth A Fletcher
Clare Furness
Brenda Gamble
Chris Hodgson
Andrew Jacko Jackson
Tony Jackson
Frankie & Byron Jacques
Bob Jobing
Frances Jones

Alistair Scott Kirby
Kevin Kitching
Michael Lee
Angus J. Lee
Alan David Oliver
Andrew Pearson
Brenda Saunders
Richard Bligh Smith
Gregory S Styles
Christopher Turner
Michael Walden
Chris Walker
Gareth Ward
Geoff Watson
Peter Watson
Graham S. Whitaker
Graham White
Dane Whittleston
Nigel R Wilson
James Wordsworth
Jane and Niall